Math

BRIGHTER CHILD

Table of Contents

Classification Fun 4
Clown Capers 5
Dot-to-Dot Fun 6
Number Words 7
Sequencing Numbers 8
Two for the Pool 9
Cookie Clues 10
Desert Trek 11
"Mouth" Math 12
Have a Ball 13
Which Place in the Race? 14
How Many Robots in All? 15
The Missing Chickens 16
Counting Up 17
Coloring by Number 18
Problem Solving 19
Hop Along Numbers 20
Leaves Leaving the Limb 21
Secrets of Subtraction 22
Subtraction Fun 23
Subtraction Facts Through 18 24
"Grrrreat" Picture 25
Facts for 10 26
Addition and Subtraction Fun 27
Big Families 28
Place Value: Ones, Tens 29
Numbers 11 Through 18 30
Numbers 40 Through 99 31

Brighter Child®
An imprint of Carson-Dellosa Publishing LLC
P.O. Box 35665
Greensboro, NC 27425 USA

© 2006 Carson-Dellosa Publishing LLC. Except as permitted under the United States Copyright Act, no part of this publication may be reproduced, stored, or distributed in any form or by any means (mechanically, electronically, recording, etc.) without the prior written consent of Carson-Dellosa Publishing LLC. Brighter Child® is an imprint of Carson-Dellosa Publishing LLC.

Printed in the USA • All rights reserved.   ISBN 978-0-7696-7612-8

04-304117784

Hundreds, Tens, and Ones	32
Count 'Em Up!	33
Place Value: Thousands	34
Adding Tens	35
2-Digit Addition	36
Prehistoric Problems	37
2-Digit Addition	38
2-Digit Subtraction: Regrouping	39
Addition and Subtraction Review	40
Adding Hundreds	41
3-Digit Addition	42
Subtracting Hundreds	43
Problem Solving	44
Multiplication	45
Multiplication	46
Multiplication	47
Problem Solving	48
Geometry	49
Shapes	50
Measurement: Inches	51
Measuring in Centimeters	52
What a Meal!	53
Graphs	54
Treasure Quest	55
Thirds and Fourths	56
Fractions: Half, Third, Fourth	57
Fractions: Half, Third, Fourth	58
Writing the Time	59
Writing the Time	60
Matching Digital and Face Clocks	61
Writing Time on the Half-Hour	62
Counting Pennies	63
Nickels: Counting by Fives	64
Dimes: Counting by Tens	65
Counting With Dimes, Nickels, and Pennies	66
Counting With Quarters, Dimes, Nickels, and Pennies	67
Making Exact Amounts of Money: Two Ways to Pay	68
Making Exact Amounts of Money: How Much More?	69
Answer Key	70–80

Name_____

Classification Fun

Directions: Write each word in the correct row at the bottom of the page.

car    pencil    chalk    radio    boat    fork

plate    friend    airplane    drum 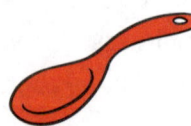   spoon    crayon

Things we ride in:

_____   _____   _____

Things we eat with:

_____   _____   _____

Things we draw with:

_____   _____   _____

Things we listen to:

_____   _____   _____

Name _____

Clown Capers

Directions: Count the number of each thing in the picture. Write the number on the line.

_____ 🎩

_____ 👞

_____ 🌸

_____ ☁

_____ △

_____ ⬭

_____ ♡

_____ ⬯

_____ ◇

_____ ☆

Name_____

Dot-to-Dot Fun

Directions: Connect the dots. Color the creature.

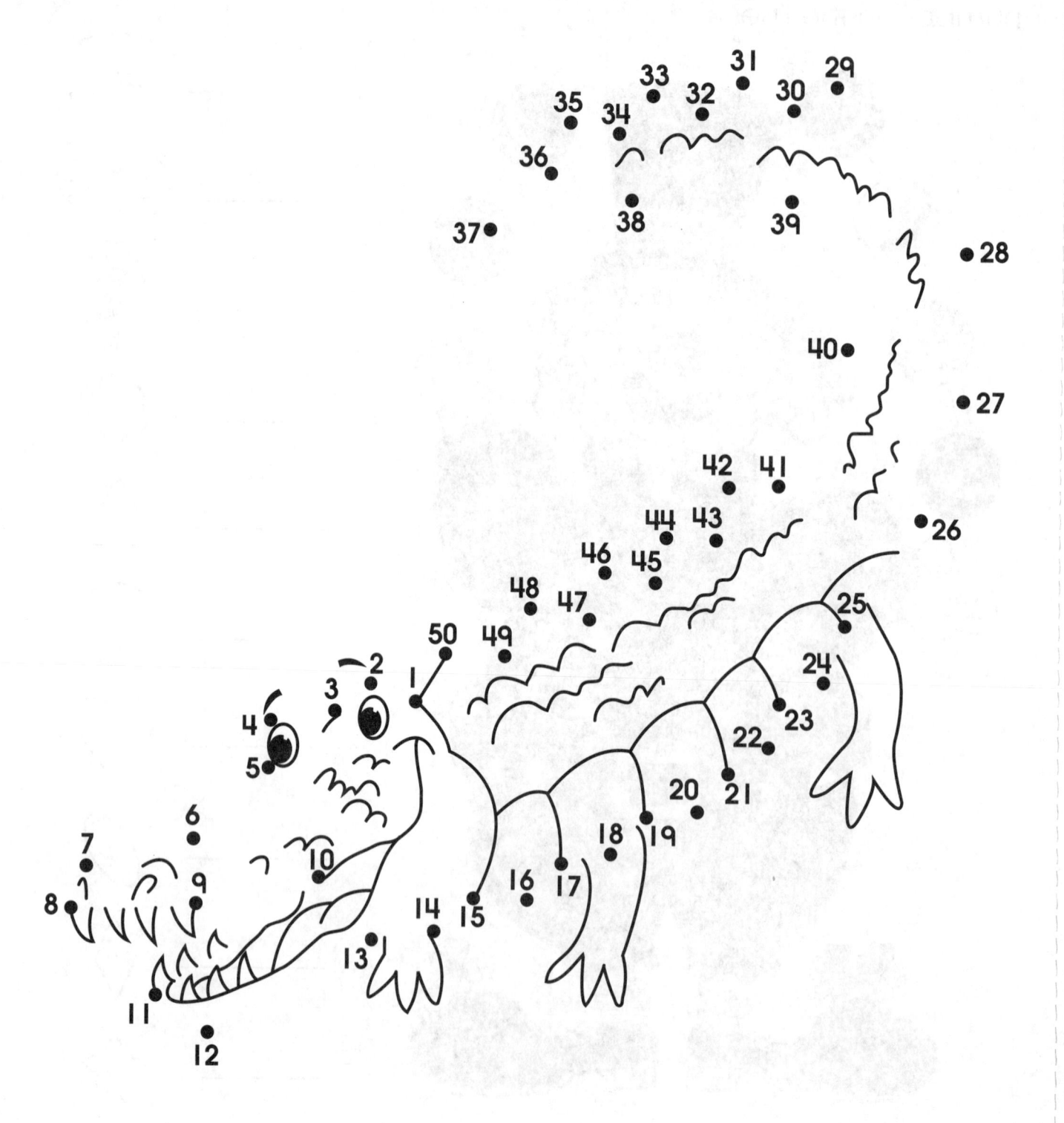

Math: Grade 2 — 6 — ©2006 Carson-Dellosa Publishing

Name _____

Number Words

Directions: Write each number beside the correct picture. Then, write it again.

| one | two | three | four | five | six | seven | eight | nine | ten |

Example:

six   six

7

Math: Grade 2

©2006 Carson-Dellosa Publishing

Name _____

Sequencing Numbers

Sequencing is putting numbers in the correct order.

Directions: Write the missing numbers.

Example: 4, __5__, 6

3, ____, 5   7, ____, 9   8, ____, 10

6, ____, 8   ____, 3, 4   ____, 5, 6

5, 6, ____   ____, 6, 7   ____, 3, 4

____, 9, 10   ____, 7, 8   2, ____, 4

2, 3, ____   1, 2, ____   7, 8, ____

2, ____, 4   ____, 7, 8   4, ____, 6

6, 7, ____   2, 3, ____   1, ____, 3

7, 8, ____   ____, 3, 4   ____, 9, 10

Math: Grade 2   ©2006 Carson-Dellosa Publishing

Name _____

Two for the Pool

Directions: Count by **2**s. Write the numbers to **30** in the water drops. Begin at the top of the slide and go down.

Name _____

Cookie Clues

Directions: Find out what holds something good! Count by **5**s to connect the dots. Color the picture.

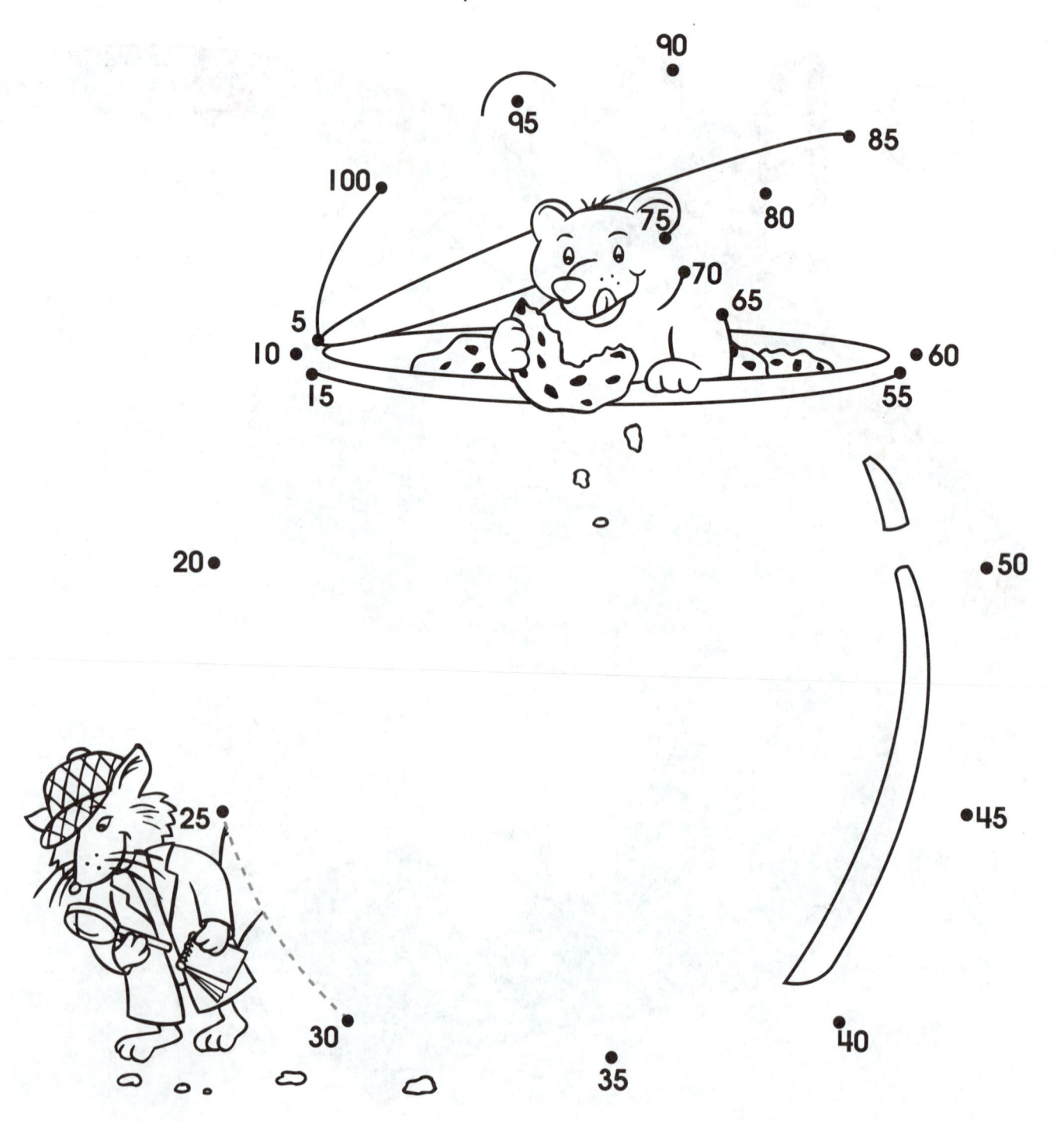

Math: Grade 2   10   ©2006 Carson-Dellosa Publishing

Name _____

Desert Trek

Directions: Count by **10**s. Color each canteen with a **10** to lead the camel to the watering hole.

©2006 Carson-Dellosa Publishing   11   Math: Grade 2

"Mouth" Math

Directions: Write **<** or **>** in each circle. Make sure the "mouth" is open toward the greater number!

36 ◯ 49   35 ◯ 53

20 ◯ 18   74 ◯ 21

53 ◯ 76   68 ◯ 80

29 ◯ 26   45 ◯ 19

90 ◯ 89   70 ◯ 67

Math: Grade 2

Name _____

Have a Ball!

Directions: Color the second ball **brown**.

Color the sixth ball **yellow**.

Color the fourth ball **orange**.

Color the first ball **black**.

Color the fifth ball **green**.

Color the seventh ball **purple**.

©2006 Carson-Dellosa Publishing   13   Math: Grade 2

Name _____

Which Place in the Race?

Directions: Write the correct word to tell each runner's place in the race.

first second third fourth fifth sixth seventh

Math: Grade 2 ©2006 Carson-Dellosa Publishing

How Many Robots in All?

Directions: Look at the pictures. Complete the addition sentences.

Example:
How many 🤖s are there in all?
2 + 4 = 6

How many  🤖s are there in all?
3 + 5 = ___

How many  🤖s are there in all?
4 + 3 = ___

How many  🤖s are there in all?
4 + 1 = ___

How many  🤖s are there in all?
2 + 5 = ___

How many  🤖s are there in all?
4 + 4 = ___

©2006 Carson-Dellosa Publishing • 15 • Math: Grade 2

Name _____

The Missing Chickens

Directions: Draw the missing pictures. Complete the addition sentences.

Example:

___ + 2 = 3

___ + 3 = 6

5 + ___ = 7

___ + 3 = 5

___ + 4 = 8

7 + ___ = 8

Math: Grade 2   ©2006 Carson-Dellosa Publishing

Name _____

Counting Up

Directions: Count up to get the sum. Write the missing addend in each blank.

3 + ___ = 6
4 + ___ = 5
7 + ___ = 9
2 + ___ = 4
3 + ___ = 8
5 + ___ = 5
8 + ___ = 10
7 + ___ = 8
6 + ___ = 9

8 + ___ = 9
4 + ___ = 6
6 + ___ = 6
5 + ___ = 7
4 + ___ = 7
9 + ___ = 10
5 + ___ = 8
7 + ___ = 10
6 + ___ = 8

©2006 Carson-Dellosa Publishing

Math: Grade 2

Name _____

Coloring by Number

Directions: Find each sum.
If the sum is **13**, color the space brown.
If the sum is **14**, color the space yellow.
If the sum is **16**, color the space red.
If the sum is **17**, color the space blue.

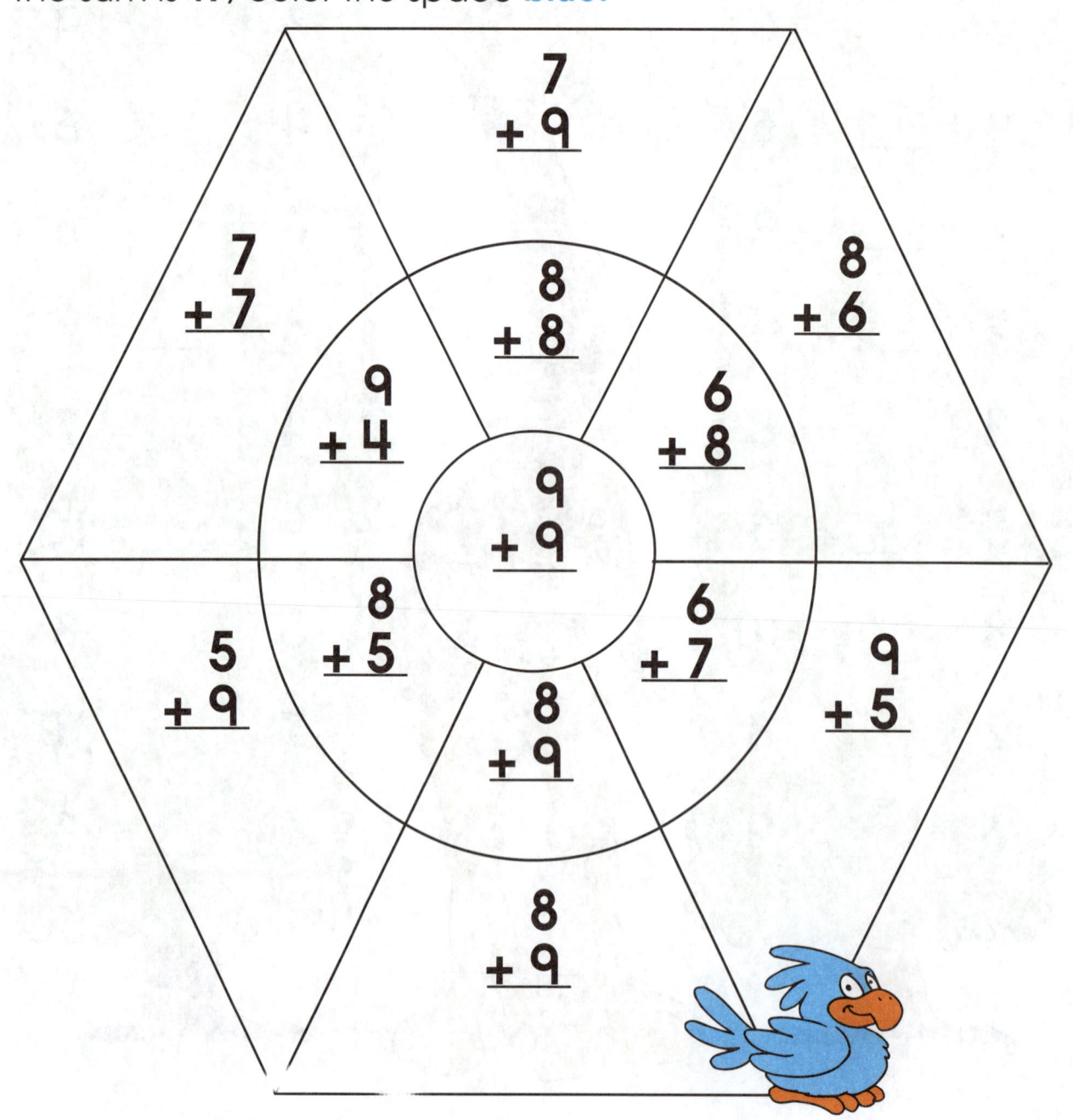

7 + 9
7 + 7
8 + 8
8 + 6
9 + 4
6 + 8
9 + 9
5 + 9
8 + 5
6 + 7
9 + 5
8 + 9
8 + 9

Math: Grade 2

Name _____

Problem Solving

Directions: Solve each problem.

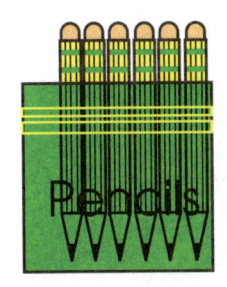

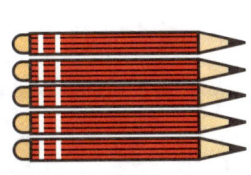

$$\begin{array}{r} 6 \\ + 5 \\ \hline \end{array}$$ pencils in a box
more pencils
pencils in all

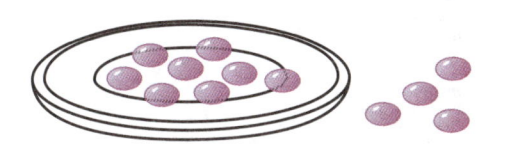

___ grapes on a plate
___ more grapes
___ grapes in all

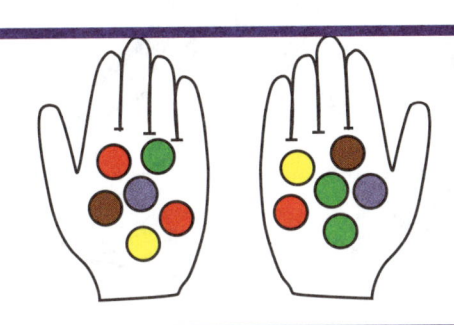

___ marbles in one hand
___ marbles in the other hand
___ marbles in all

___ people at the table
___ more people coming in
___ people in all

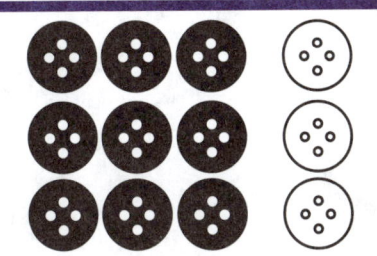

___ black buttons
___ white buttons
___ buttons in all

Name _____

Hop Along Numbers

Directions: Use the number line to count back.

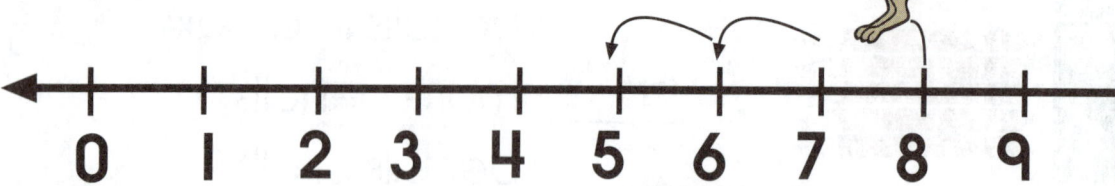

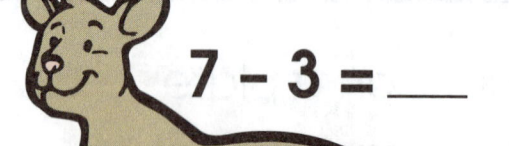

Example: 8, _7_, _6_

0 1 2 3 4 5 6 7 8 9 10

7 − 3 = ___
7, ___, ___, ___

6 − 2 = ___
6, ___, ___

8 − 1 = ___
8, ___

7 − 2 = ___
7, ___, ___

Math: Grade 2 20 ©2006 Carson-Dellosa Publishing

Name_____

Leaves Leaving the Limb

Directions: Subtract to find the difference. Use the code to color the leaves. Code: **0 = green**   **1 = red**   **2 = yellow**   **3 = brown**

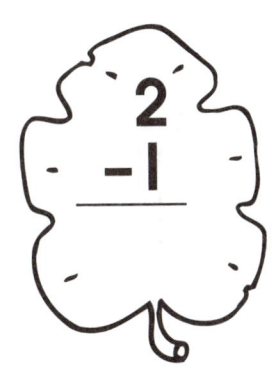

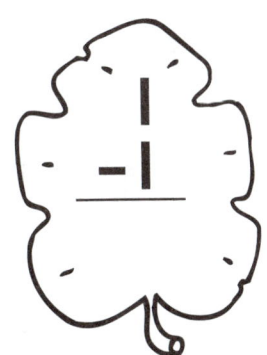

$\begin{array}{r} 1 \\ -0 \\ \hline \end{array}$ $\begin{array}{r} 5 \\ -2 \\ \hline \end{array}$ $\begin{array}{r} 3 \\ -3 \\ \hline \end{array}$ $\begin{array}{r} 2 \\ -1 \\ \hline \end{array}$

$\begin{array}{r} 3 \\ -1 \\ \hline \end{array}$ $\begin{array}{r} 2 \\ -2 \\ \hline \end{array}$ $\begin{array}{r} 4 \\ -2 \\ \hline \end{array}$ $\begin{array}{r} 5 \\ -3 \\ \hline \end{array}$

$\begin{array}{r} 3 \\ -0 \\ \hline \end{array}$ $\begin{array}{r} 5 \\ -4 \\ \hline \end{array}$ $\begin{array}{r} 1 \\ -1 \\ \hline \end{array}$ $\begin{array}{r} 2 \\ -1 \\ \hline \end{array}$

How many of each color?

_____   _____   _____   _____

Name_____

Secrets of Subtraction

Directions: Solve the subtraction problems. Use the code to find the secret message.

Code:

7	5	2	6	4	3
K	T	Y	E	W	A

PLEASE, DON'T EVER

8	10	9	10
-3	-7	-2	-4

9	6	7	8
-6	-2	-4	-6

MY MATH!

Math: Grade 2

Name _____

Subtraction Fun

Directions: Subtract to find each difference.

10	7	9	8	10
− 5	− 2	− 8	− 4	− 10

8	7	10	9	9
− 3	− 6	− 3	− 7	− 1

9	6	10	8	10
− 6	− 3	− 9	− 5	− 4

©2006 Carson-Dellosa Publishing

Math: Grade 2

Name_____

Subtraction Facts Through 18

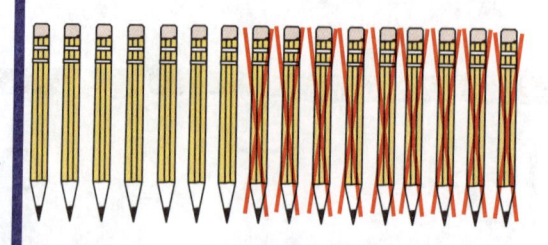

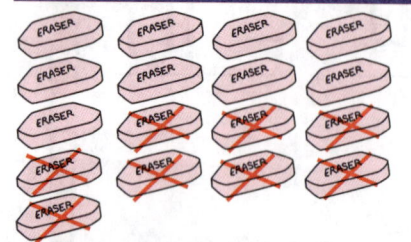

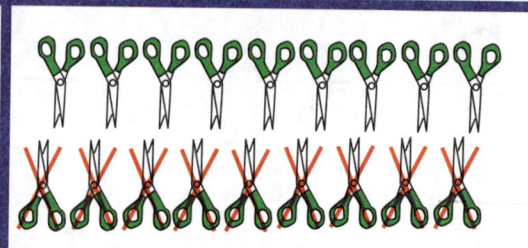

Directions: Subtract.
Example:

15
− 7
―――
8

16
− 9
―――

17
− 8
―――

18
− 9
―――

Directions: Subtract.

18	13	16	17	14	13
− 9	− 5	− 8	− 9	− 6	− 9

17	15	14	13	16	12
− 8	− 9	− 5	− 6	− 7	− 4

14	15	16	12	15	13
− 7	− 8	− 9	− 7	− 7	− 4

15	14	12	13	14	11
− 6	− 8	− 3	− 9	− 9	− 3

Math: Grade 2   ©2006 Carson-Dellosa Publishing

Name _____

"Grrreat" Picture

Directions: Subtract. Write the answer in the space. Then, color the spaces according to the answers.

1 = white   2 = purple   3 = black   4 = green   5 = yellow
6 = blue   7 = pink   8 = gray   9 = orange   10 = red

©2006 Carson-Dellosa Publishing   25   Math: Grade 2

Name_____

Facts for 10

Directions: Add or subtract.

Examples:

```
  5        6       4        7       3
+ 5      + 4     + 6      + 3     + 7
 10
```

```
 10       10      10       10      10
- 5      - 4     - 6      - 3     - 7
  5
```

```
  8        2       9        1
+ 2      + 8     + 1      + 9
```

```
 10       10      10       10
- 2      - 8     - 1      - 9
```

```
  4        5       9       10       10      10
+ 6      + 5     + 1      - 8      - 3     - 0
```

Math: Grade 2   26   ©2006 Carson-Dellosa Publishing

Name _____

Addition and Subtraction Fun

Directions: Solve the number problem under each picture. Write **+** or **−** to show if you should add or subtract.

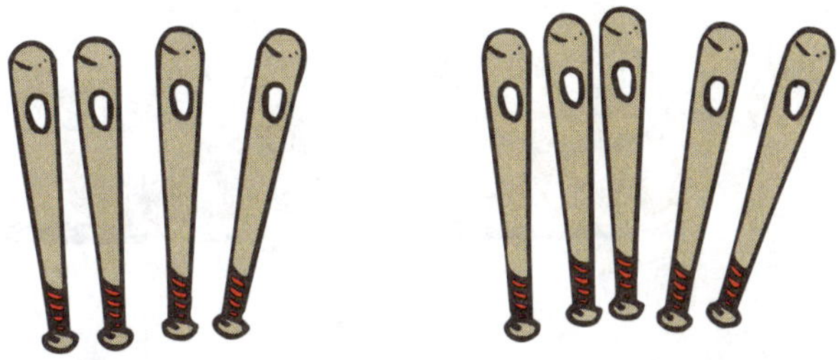

Example:

How many 🏏s in all?

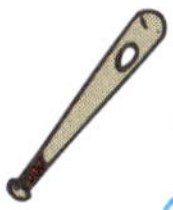

4 + 5 = 9

How many  🍫s in all?

7   5 = _____

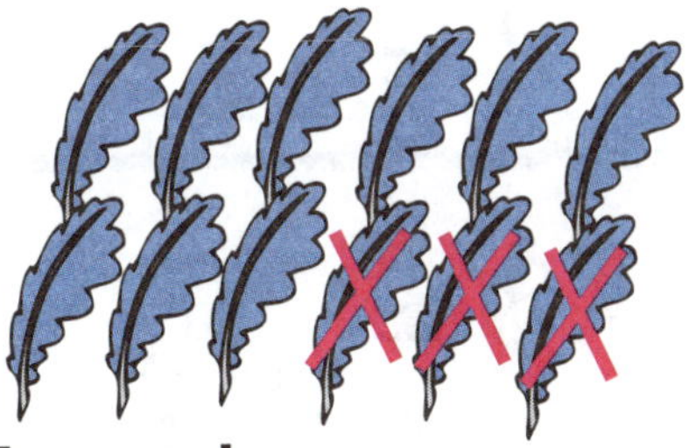

Example:

How many 🪶s are left?

12 − 3 = 9

How many  ⭐s are left?

15   8 = _____

How many  🍬s in all?

5   8 = _____

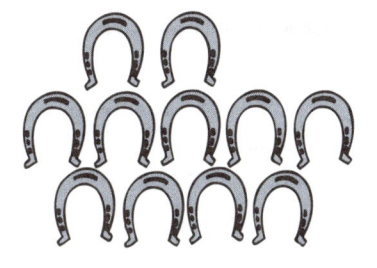

How many  🧲s are left?

11   4 = _____

©2006 Carson-Dellosa Publishing   27   Math: Grade 2

Big Families

Directions: Complete each number sentence in each number family.

2
0 + ___ = 2
2 + 0 = ___
___ − 0 = 2
2 − 2 = ___

3
1 + 2 = ___
___ + 1 = 3
3 − ___ = 2
3 − 2 = ___

4
___ + 3 = 4
3 + 1 = ___
4 − ___ = 3
___ − 3 = 1

5
2 + 3 = ___
___ + 2 = 5
5 − ___ = 3
___ − 3 = 2

6
2 + ___ = 6
4 + 2 = ___
6 − ___ = 4
6 − 4 = ___

6
5 + ___ = 6
___ + ___ = ___
6 − ___ = 5
___ − 5 = ___

Math: Grade 2

Name _____

Place Value: Ones, Tens

The **place value** of a digit or numeral is shown by where it is in the number. For example, in the number **23**, **2** has the place value of **tens**, and **3** is **ones**.

Directions: Add the tens and ones and write your answers in the blanks.

Example:

3 tens + 3 ones = 33

                        tens ones   tens ones

7 tens + 5 ones = _____   4 tens + 0 ones = _____

2 tens + 3 ones = _____   8 tens + 1 one = _____

5 tens + 2 ones = _____   1 ten + 1 one = _____

5 tens + 4 ones = _____   6 tens + 3 ones = _____

9 tens + 5 ones = _____

Directions: Draw a line to the correct number.

6 tens + 7 ones   73
4 tens + 2 ones   67
8 tens + 0 ones   51
7 tens + 3 ones   80
5 tens + 1 one   42

Name_____

Numbers 11 Through 18

1¢   10¢   10¢

Directions: Complete the problems.
Example:

__1__ ten __1__ one = __11__

____ ten ____ ones = ____

____ ten ____ ones = ____

____ ten ____ ones = ____

____ ten ____ ones = ____

____ ten ____ ones = ____

____ ten ____ ones = ____

____ ten ____ ones = ____

Name _____

Numbers 40 Through 99

Directions: Complete the problems.

Example:

__4__ tens __5__ ones = __45__

____ tens ____ ones = ____

____ tens = ____

____ tens ____ ones = ____

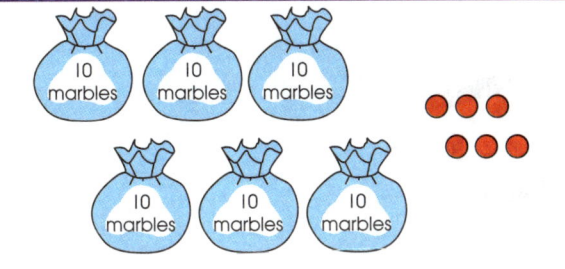

____ tens ____ ones = ____

____ tens ____ ones = ____

____ tens = ____

____ tens ____ ones = ____

Name _____

Hundreds, Tens, and Ones

Directions: Count the groups of crayons. Write the number of hundreds, tens, and ones.

Example:

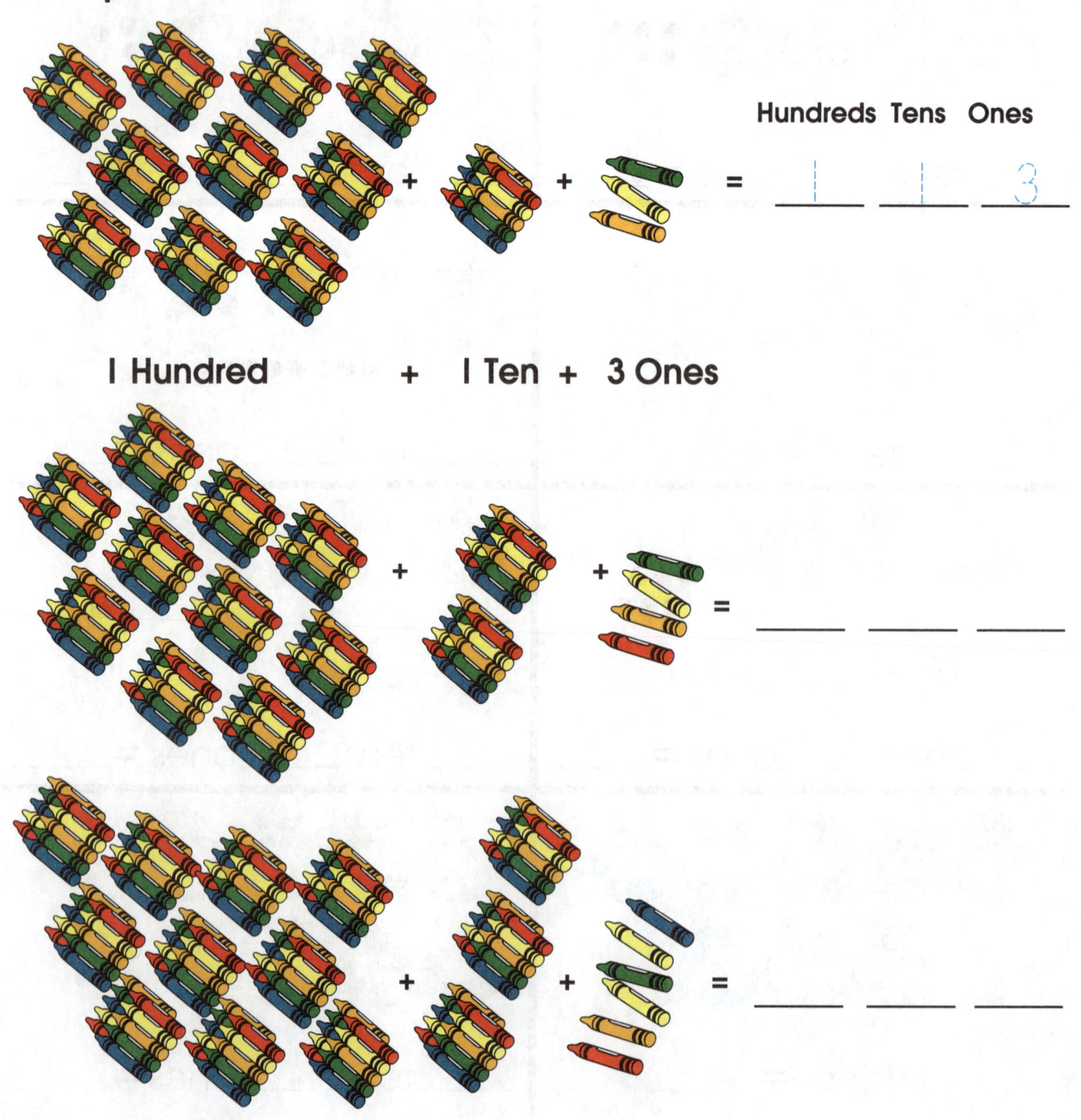

Hundreds Tens Ones
= ___1___ ___1___ ___3___

1 Hundred   +   1 Ten   +   3 Ones

+ ___ + ___ = ___ ___ ___

+ ___ + ___ = ___ ___ ___

Math: Grade 2   32   ©2006 Carson-Dellosa Publishing

Name _____

Count 'Em Up!

Directions: Look at the example. Then, write the missing numbers in the blanks.

Example:

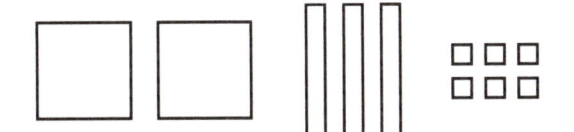

2 hundreds + 3 tens + 6 ones =

hundreds	tens	ones
2	3	6

= 236

	hundreds	tens	ones	
3 hundreds + 4 tens + 8 ones =	3	4	8	= _____
___ hundreds + ___ ten + ___ ones =	2	1	7	= _____
___ hundreds + ___ tens + ___ ones =	6	3	5	= _____
___ hundreds + ___ tens + ___ ones =	4	7	9	= _____
___ hundreds + ___ tens + ___ ones =	2	9	4	= _____
___ hundreds + ___ tens + ___ ones =	4	2	0	= _____
3 hundreds + 1 ten + 3 ones = _____	___	___	___	= _____
3 hundreds + ___ tens + 7 ones = _____		5	___	= _____
6 hundreds + 2 tens + ___ ones = _____		___	8	= _____

©2006 Carson-Dellosa Publishing   Math: Grade 2

Name _____

Place Value: Thousands

Directions: Study the example. Write the missing numbers.

Example:

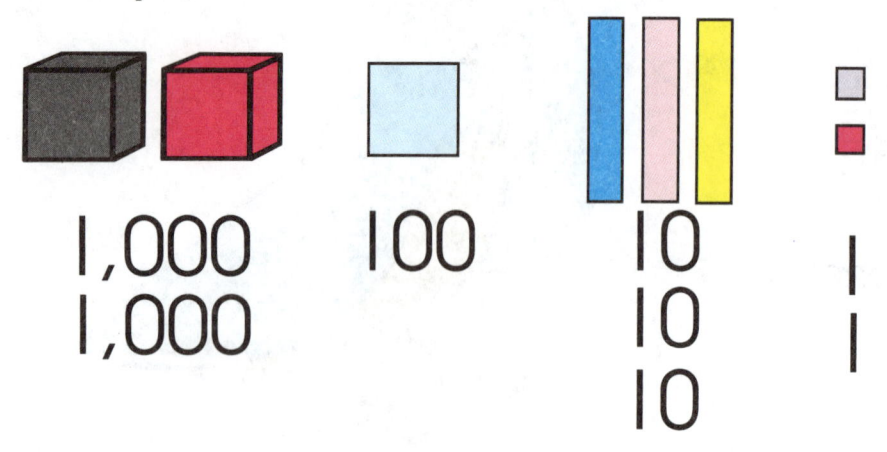

1,000   100   10   1
1,000   10   1
              10

2 thousands + 1 hundred + __3__ tens + 2 ones = __2,132__

5,286 = ___ thousands + ___ hundreds + ___ tens + ___ ones

1,831 = ___ thousand + ___ hundreds + ___ tens + ___ one

8,972 = ___ thousands + ___ hundreds + ___ tens + ___ ones

4,528 = ___ thousands + ___ hundreds + ___ tens + ___ ones

3,177 = ___ thousands + ___ hundred + ___ tens + ___ ones

Directions: Draw a line to the number that has:

8 hundreds	7,103
5 ones	2,862
9 tens	5,996
7 thousands	1,485

Math: Grade 2 ©2006 Carson-Dellosa Publishing

Name _____

Adding Tens

3 tens	30		6 tens	60
+ 4 tens	+40		+ 2 tens	+20
7 tens	70		8 tens	80

Directions: Add.

2 tens	20		6 tens	60
+ 4 tens	+40		+ 2 tens	+20
___ tens			___ tens	

20	10	40	30	50
+20	+50	+20	+40	+30

30	60	20	70	10
+20	+10	+50	+10	+10

10	40	80	60	20
+20	+40	+10	+30	+60

70	40	30	50	30
+20	+10	+10	+40	+30

©2006 Carson-Dellosa Publishing   Math: Grade 2

Name_____

2-Digit Addition

Directions: Study the example. Follow the steps to add.

Example: 33
             +41

Step 1: Add the ones.   **Step 2:** Add the tens.

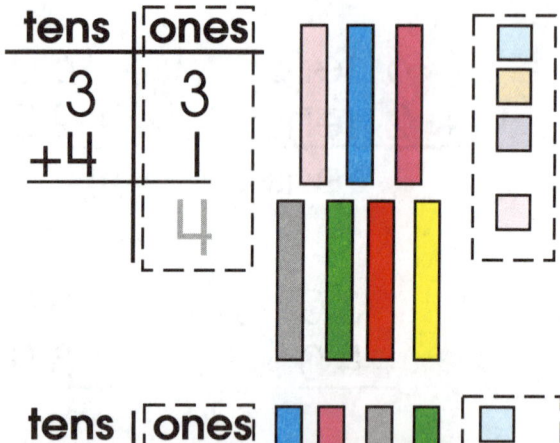

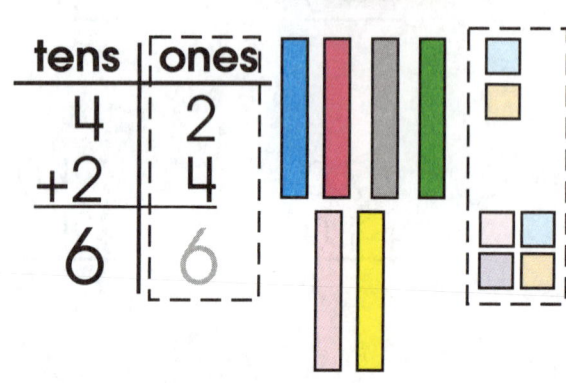

tens	ones
3	3
+4	1
	4

tens	ones
3	3
+4	1
7	4

tens	ones
4	2
+2	4
6	6

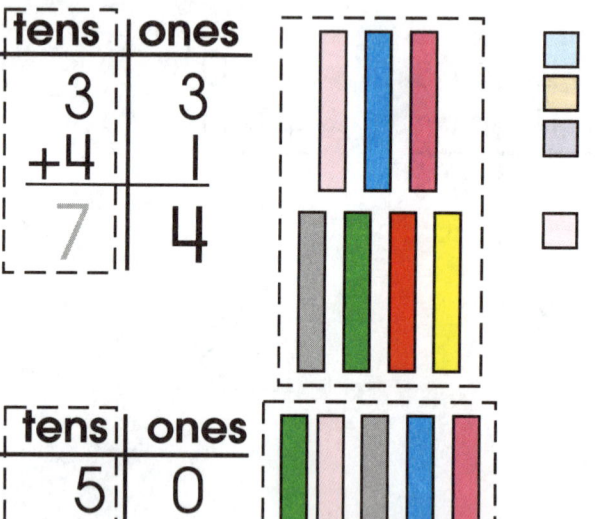

tens	ones
5	0
+4	7
9	7

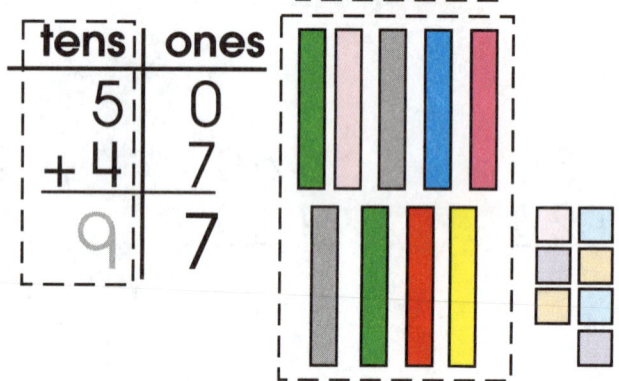

 24   15   38   11   37   72   33   10
+62   +23   +61   +26   +42   +11   +51   +30

 25   62   32   25   82   91   16   55
+42   +14   +44   +13   + 6   + 5   +71   + 3

Name _____

Prehistoric Problems

Directions: Solve the subtraction problems. Use the code to color the picture.

Code: 25 = blue   57 = green
       31 = yellow   14 = orange
       21 = brown   11 = red

47 − 22

52 − 21

25 − 11

62 − 31

77 − 20

51 − 40

69 − 12

98 − 41

55 − 34

©2006 Carson-Dellosa Publishing   37   Math: Grade 2

Name _____

2-Digit Addition

Directions: Add the ones.   Rename 15 as 10 + 5.   Add the tens.

```
  56          6              1            1
 +29         +9             56           56
            ———            +29          +29
            15 or 10 + 5 ——→  5           85
```

Directions: Add the ones.   Rename 12 as 10 + 2.   Add the tens.

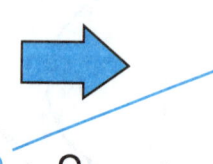

```
  47          7              1            1
 +35         +5             47           47
            ———            +35          +35
            12 or 10 + 2 ——→  2           82
```

Directions: Add.

Examples:

```
  45         13         48         69         54
 +28        +19        +35        +18        +39
 ———        ———
  73         32
```

```
  44         37         28         73         66
 +17        +18        +36        +18        +29
```

```
  52         38         64         29         75
 +39        +47        +18        +45        +17
```

Math: Grade 2   38   ©2006 Carson-Dellosa Publishing

Name _____

2-Digit Subtraction: Regrouping

Subtraction is "taking away" or subtracting one number from another to find the difference. Regrouping is using **one ten** to form **ten ones**, **one 100** to form **ten tens**, and so on.

Directions: Study the examples. Follow the steps to subtract.

Example: 37
              −19

Step 1: Regroup.

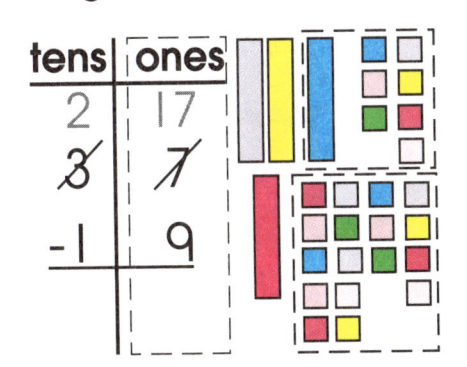

Step 2: Subtract the ones.

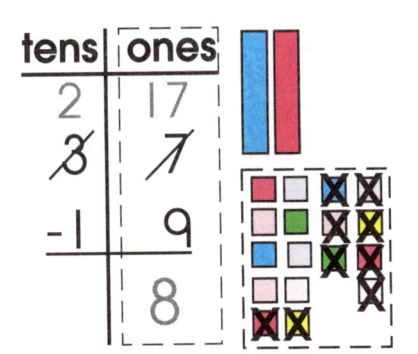

Step 3: Subtract the tens.

| 28 | 46 | 12 | 30 | 52 | 47 | 21 | 45 |
| −19 | −18 | − 8 | −12 | −25 | −35 | −13 | −25 |

©2006 Carson-Dellosa Publishing   39   Math: Grade 2

Name_____

Addition and Subtraction Review

Directions: Add.

4	8	9	7	5	6
+ 9	+ 6	+ 8	+ 6	+ 7	+ 5

9	5	7	9	8	7
+ 6	+ 8	+ 4	+ 9	+ 7	+ 9

30	20	45	52	60	83
+ 40	+ 30	+ 23	+ 23	+ 25	+ 15

Directions: Subtract.

16	15	13	12	11	17
− 7	− 9	− 4	− 7	− 9	− 8

18	17	16	15	4	16
− 9	− 9	− 8	− 8	− 7	− 9

40	60	85	73	96	54
− 30	− 10	− 23	− 41	− 43	− 44

Math: Grade 2   40   ©2006 Carson-Dellosa Publishing

Adding Hundreds

Examples:

```
  5 hundreds        5 0 0         4 hundreds        4 0 0
+ 3 hundreds      + 3 0 0       + 5 hundreds      + 5 0 0
  8 hundreds        8 0 0         9 hundreds        9 0 0
```

Directions: Add.

```
  3 hundreds       3 0 0          6 hundreds        6 0 0
+ 1 hundreds     + 1 0 0        + 2 hundreds      + 2 0 0
  4 hundreds       4 0 0            hundreds
```

```
   2 0 0           1 0 0             6 0 0            4 0 0
 + 2 0 0         + 7 0 0           + 3 0 0          + 5 0 0
```

```
   3 0 0           8 0 0             4 0 0            7 0 0
 + 4 0 0         + 1 0 0           + 4 0 0          + 2 0 0
```

```
   5 0 0           1 0 0             5 0 0            3 0 0
 + 1 0 0         + 6 0 0           + 2 0 0          + 2 0 0
```

```
   3 0 0           4 0 0             3 0 0            2 0 0
 + 3 0 0         + 2 0 0           + 5 0 0          + 1 0 0
```

Name _____

3-Digit Addition

```
   2 4 5          2 4 5          2 4 5
+  2 5 3       +  2 5 3       +  2 5 3
  ─────          ─────          ─────
      8            9 8          4 9 8
```

Directions: Add.

Example:

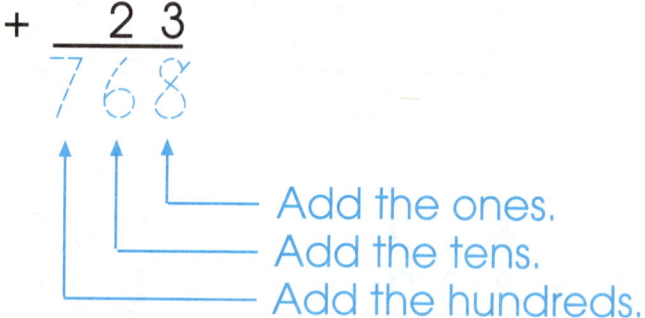

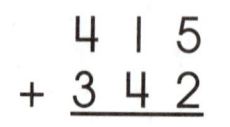

```
   7 4 5                    6 2 3
+    2 3                 +  1 5 6
  ─────                    ─────
   7 6 8
```

↑ ↑ ↑ — Add the ones.   ↑ ↑ ↑ — Add the ones.
  └─── Add the tens.   └─── Add the tens.
    └── Add the hundreds.   └── Add the hundreds.

```
   4 1 5       5 6 6         3 7 3        1 6 0
+  3 4 2    +    3 3      +  2 2 1     +  3 3 4
  ─────       ─────          ─────        ─────


   8 3 5       6 4 2         2 8 7        7 2 3
+    4 2    +  2 5 1      +  4 1 2     +    4 5
  ─────       ─────          ─────        ─────


   1 3 3       4 5 4         3 1 4        6 5 4
+  5 2 2    +  3 2 4      +  6 0 2     +  2 3 5
  ─────       ─────          ─────        ─────
```

Math: Grade 2   42   ©2006 Carson-Dellosa Publishing

Name _____

Subtracting Hundreds

```
  8 hundreds      800        6 hundreds      600
- 3 hundreds    - 300      - 2 hundreds    - 200
  5 hundreds      500        4 hundreds      400
```

Directions: Subtract.

Example:

```
  9 hundreds      900        3 hundreds      300
- 7 hundreds    - 700      - 1 hundreds    - 100
  2 hundreds      200          hundreds
```

```
  700       500       900       800
- 300     - 400     - 400     - 500
```

```
  600       300       500       400
- 500     - 200     - 100     - 200
```

```
  900       800       600       500
- 100     - 400     - 200     - 300
```

```
  400       700       800       900
- 100     - 600     - 200     - 600
```

©2006 Carson-Dellosa Publishing Math: Grade 2

Name_____

Problem Solving

Directions: Solve each problem.

Example:

The grocery store buys 568 cans of beans.

It sells 345 cans of beans.

How many cans of beans are left?

$$568 - 345 = 223$$

The cooler holds 732 gallons of milk.

It has 412 gallons of milk in it.

How many more gallons of milk will it take to fill the cooler?

Ann does 635 push-ups.

Carl does 421 push-ups.

How many more push-ups does Ann do?

Kurt has 386 pennies.

Neal has 32 pennies.

How many more pennies does Kurt have?

It takes 874 nails to build a tree house.

Jillian has 532 nails.

How many more nails does she need?

Name _____

Multiplication

Multiplication is a short way to find the sum of adding the same number a certain amount of times. For example, 7 x 4 = 28 instead of 7 + 7 + 7 + 7 = 28.

Directions: Study the example. Solve the problems.

Example:
3 + 3 + 3 = 9
3 threes = 9
3 x 3 = 9

7 + 7 = ____
2 sevens = ____
2 x 7 = ____

4 + 4 + 4 + 4 = ____
4 fours = ____
4 x ____ = ____

5 + 5 = ____
2 fives = ____
2 x ____ = ____

2 + 2 + 2 + 2 = ____
4 twos = ____
4 x ____ = ____

6 + 6 = ____
2 sixes = ____
2 x ____ = ____

©2006 Carson-Dellosa Publishing

45

Math: Grade 2

Multiplication

Directions: Solve the problems.

9 + 9 = ____

2 nines = ____

2 x 9 = ____

7 + 7 = ____

2 sevens = ____

2 x ____ = ____

Multiplication saves time. It's faster than addition!

4 + 4 + 4 + 4 = ____

____ fours = ____

____ x 4 = ____

8 + 8 + 8 + 8 + 8 = ____

____ eights = ____

____ x 8 = ____

5 + 5 + 5 = ____

____ fives = ____

____ x 5 = ____

9 + 9 = ____

____ nines = ____

____ x 9 = ____

6 + 6 + 6 = ____

____ sixes = ____

____ x 6 = ____

3 + 3 = ____

____ threes = ____

____ x 3 = ____

7 + 7 + 7 + 7 = ____

____ sevens = ____

____ x 7 = ____

2 + 2 = ____

____ twos = ____

____ x 2 = ____

Name _____

Multiplication

Directions: Use the code to color the fish.

If the answer is:

6, color it **red**.

12, color it **orange**.

16, color it **blue**.

27, color it **brown**.

8, color it **yellow**.

15, color it **green**.

18, color it **purple**.

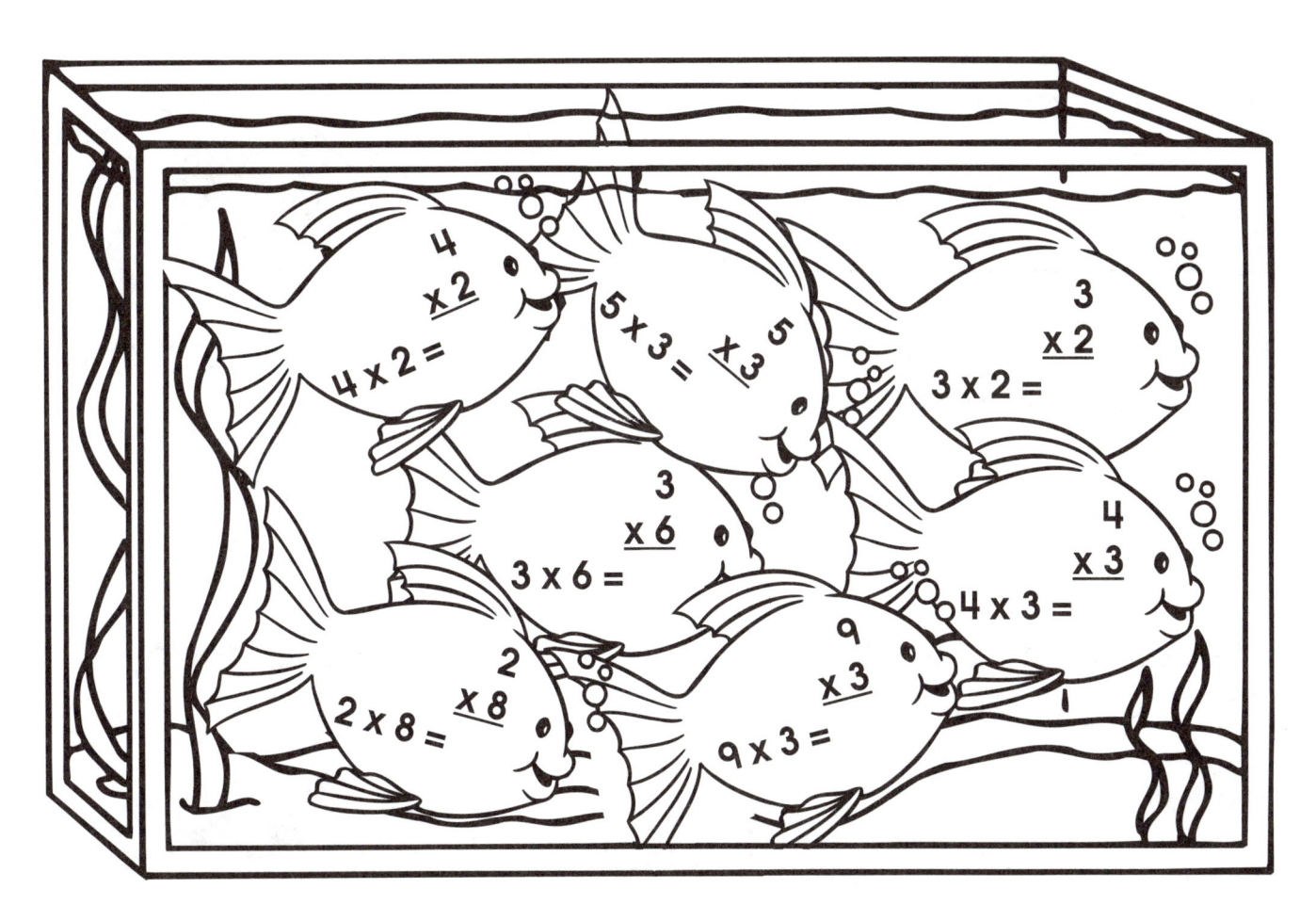

$4 \times 2 =$

$5 \times 3 =$

$3 \times 2 =$

$3 \times 6 =$

$4 \times 3 =$

$2 \times 8 =$

$9 \times 3 =$

Problem Solving

Directions: Tell if you add, subtract, or multiply. Then, write the answers. Hints: "In all" means to add. "Left" means to subtract. Groups with the same number in each means to multiply.

Example:

There are 6 red birds and 7 blue birds. How many birds in all?

____add____ ____13____ birds

The pet store had 25 goldfish, but 10 were sold. How many goldfish are left?

_____ _____ goldfish

There are 5 cages of bunnies. There are two bunnies in each cage. How many bunnies are there in the store?

_____ _____ bunnies

The store had 18 puppies this morning. It sold 7 puppies today. How many puppies are left?

_____ _____ puppies

Name _____

Geometry

Geometry is mathematics that has to do with lines and shapes.

Directions: Color the shapes.

Color the triangles **blue.**
Color the circles **red.**
Color the squares **green.**
Color the rectangles **pink.**

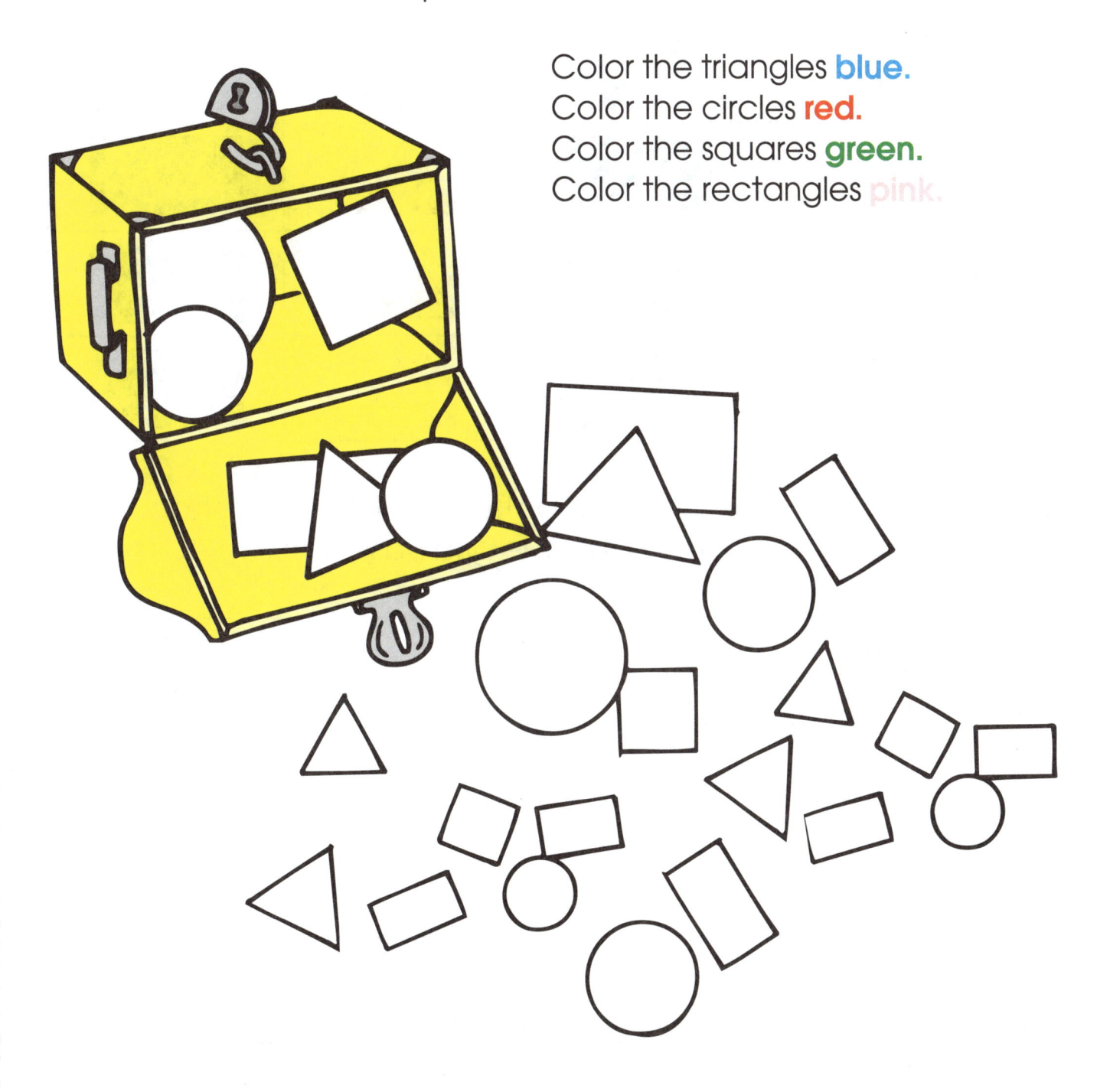

©2006 Carson-Dellosa Publishing 49 Math: Grade 2

Name _____

Shapes

Directions: Look at the grid below. All the shapes have straight sides, like a square.

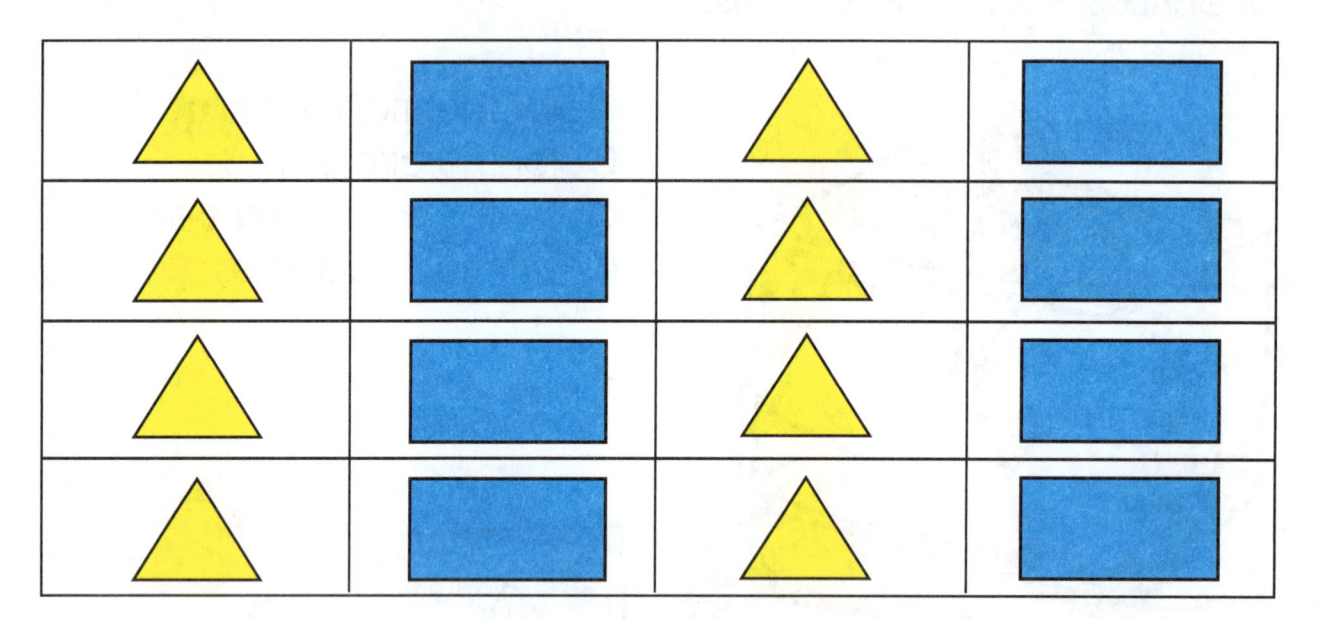

Directions: Now, make your own pattern grid. Use only shapes with straight sides like the grid above. The grid has been started for you.

Math: Grade 2   ©2006 Carson-Dellosa Publishing

Name _____

Measurement: Inches

An **inch** is a unit of length in the standard measurement system.

Directions: Use the ruler on pg. 203 to measure each object to the nearest inch.

Example: The paper clip is about 1 inch long.

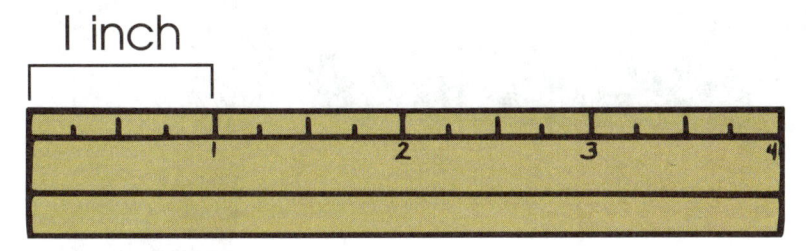

about __1__ inches

about ____ inches

about ____ inches

about ____ inches

about ____ inches

about ____ inches

about ____ inches

©2006 Carson-Dellosa Publishing   51   Math: Grade 2

Name_____

Measuring in Centimeters

Directions: Use a centimeter ruler to find the height or the length of the objects below. Write the answer in each blank.

Example:

14 cm

centimeters

_____ cm

_____ cm

_____ cm

_____ cm

_____ cm

Math: Grade 2 52 ©2006 Carson-Dellosa Publishing

Name _____

What a Meal!

Directions: Use the pictograph to complete each sentence below.

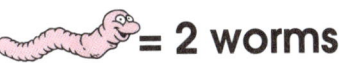

🪱 = 2 worms

Grace Goldfish	🪱 🪱 🪱 🪱
Willie Walleye	🪱 🪱 🪱 🪱 🪱 🪱 🪱
Calvin Catfish	🪱 🪱 🪱 🪱 🪱
Benny Bluegill	🪱 🪱 🪱
Beth Bass	🪱 🪱 🪱 🪱 🪱 🪱 🪱
Patty Perch	🪱 🪱 🪱 🪱

1. _____ got the fewest worms.

2. _____ got the most worms.

3. _____ and _____ got the same number of worms.

4. Benny and Patty together caught the same number of worms as _____ .

5. Write the number of worms that each fish ate.

____ ____ ____ ____ ____ ____
Grace Willie Calvin Benny Beth Patty

©2006 Carson-Dellosa Publishing   Math: Grade 2

Name _____

Graphs

Directions: Count the banana peels in each column. Color the boxes to show how many bananas have been eaten by the monkeys.

Example:

Math: Grade 2   54   ©2006 Carson-Dellosa Publishing

Name _____

Treasure Quest

Directions: Read the directions. Draw the pictures where they belong on the grid. Start at 0 and go . . .

over 2, up 5. Draw a

over 9, up 3. Draw a

over 8, up 6. Draw a

over 5, up 2. Draw a

over 1, up 7. Draw a

over 7, up 1. Draw a

over 6, up 4. Draw a

over 2, up 3. Draw a

over 3, up 1. Draw a

over 4, up 6. Draw a

©2006 Carson-Dellosa Publishing 55 Math: Grade 2

Name_____

Thirds and Fourths

Directions: Each shape has **3** equal parts. Color one section, or $\frac{1}{3}$, of each shape.

Directions: Each shape has **4** equal parts. Color one section, or $\frac{1}{4}$, of each shape.

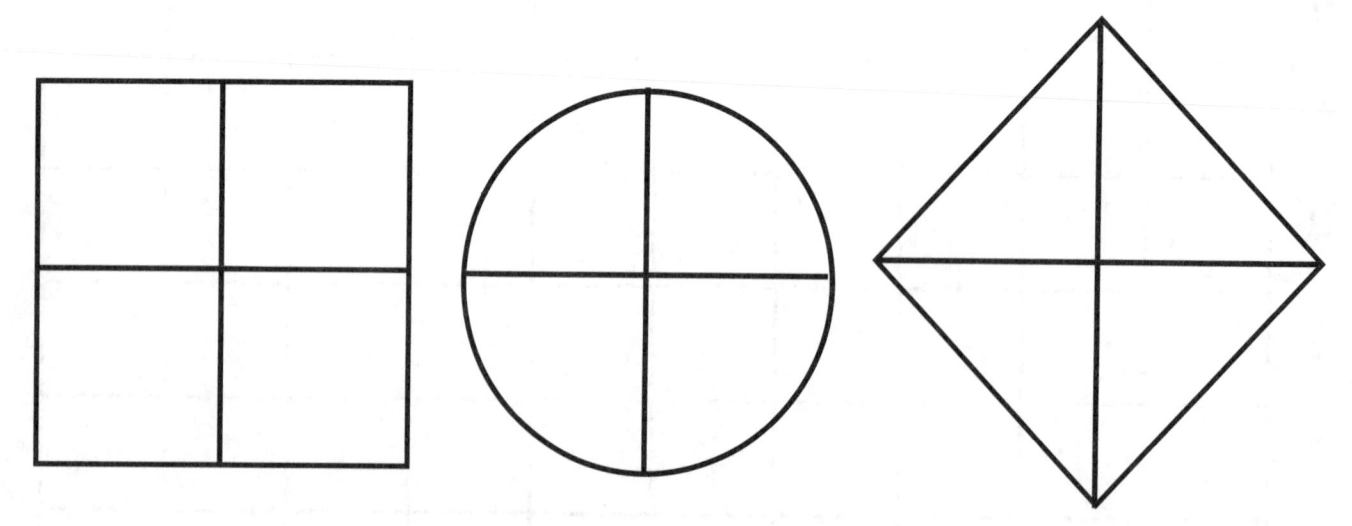

Math: Grade 2 ©2006 Carson-Dellosa Publishing

Name _____

Fractions: Half, Third, Fourth

Directions: Color the correct fraction of each shape.

Examples:

shaded part 1
equal parts 2
$\frac{1}{2}$ (one-half)

shaded part 1
equal parts 3
$\frac{1}{3}$ (one-third)

shaded part 1
equal parts 4
$\frac{1}{4}$ (one-fourth)

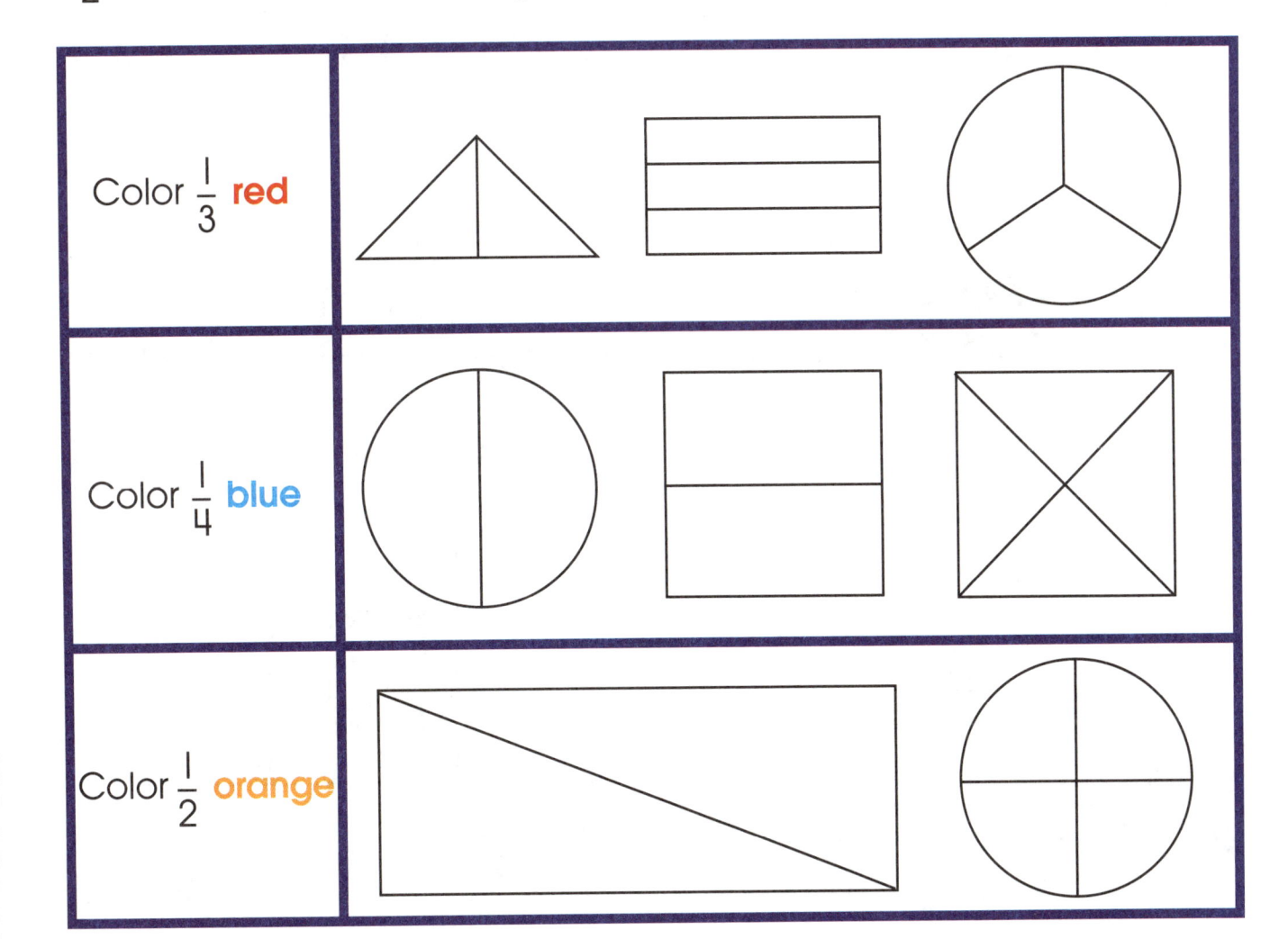

Color $\frac{1}{3}$ red

Color $\frac{1}{4}$ blue

Color $\frac{1}{2}$ orange

©2006 Carson-Dellosa Publishing   57   Math: Grade 2

Name _____

Fractions: Half, Third, Fourth

Directions: Study the examples. Circle the fraction that shows the shaded part. Then, circle the fraction that shows the white part.

Examples:

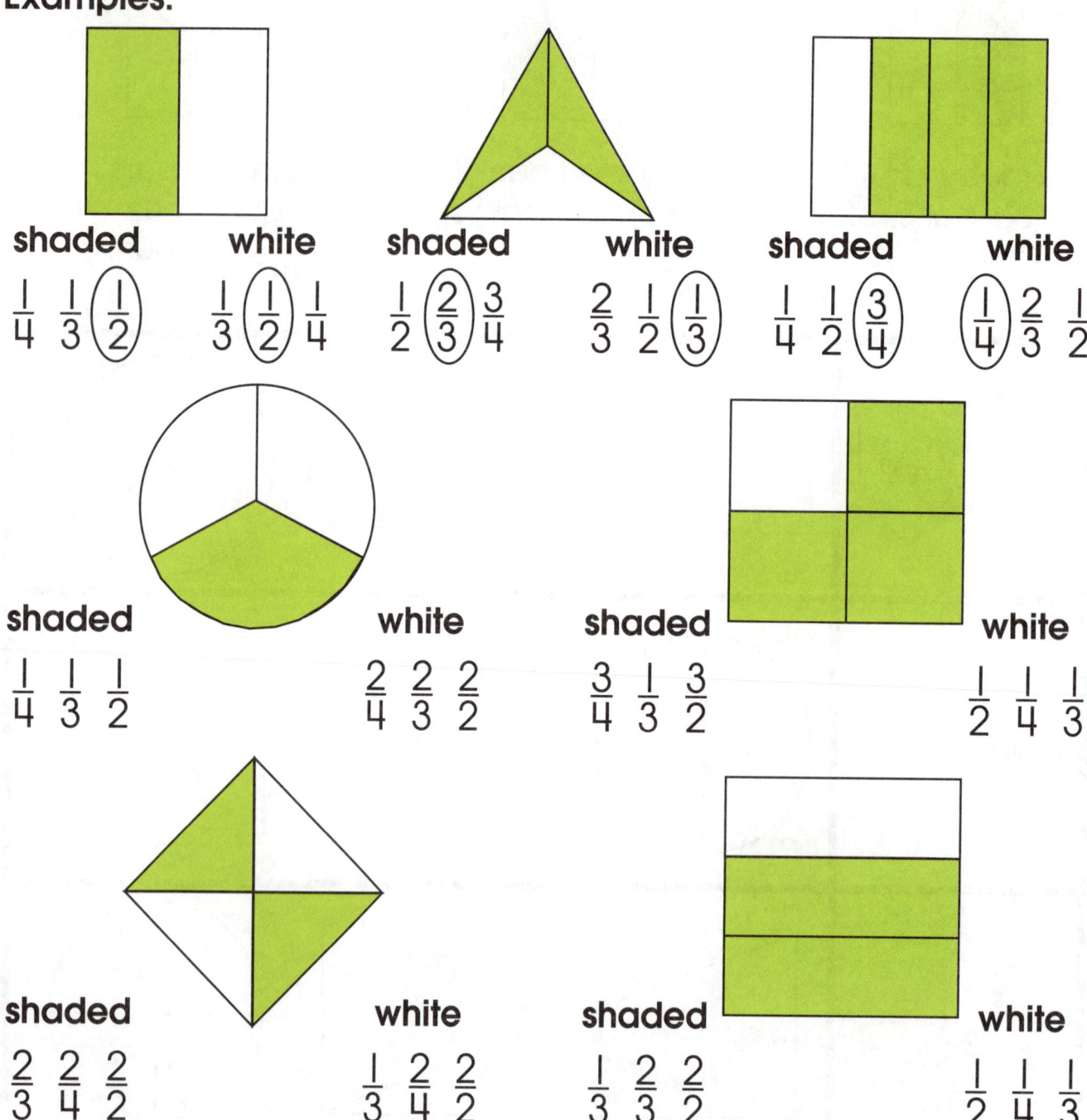

shaded   white
$\frac{1}{4}$ $\frac{1}{3}$ $\textcircled{\frac{1}{2}}$ $\frac{1}{3}$ $\textcircled{\frac{1}{2}}$ $\frac{1}{4}$

shaded   white
$\frac{1}{2}$ $\textcircled{\frac{2}{3}}$ $\frac{3}{4}$ $\frac{2}{3}$ $\frac{1}{2}$ $\textcircled{\frac{1}{3}}$

shaded   white
$\frac{1}{4}$ $\frac{1}{2}$ $\textcircled{\frac{3}{4}}$ $\textcircled{\frac{1}{4}}$ $\frac{2}{3}$ $\frac{1}{2}$

shaded   white
$\frac{1}{4}$ $\frac{1}{3}$ $\frac{1}{2}$ $\frac{2}{4}$ $\frac{2}{3}$ $\frac{2}{2}$

shaded   white
$\frac{3}{4}$ $\frac{1}{3}$ $\frac{3}{2}$ $\frac{1}{2}$ $\frac{1}{4}$ $\frac{1}{3}$

shaded   white
$\frac{2}{3}$ $\frac{2}{4}$ $\frac{2}{2}$ $\frac{1}{3}$ $\frac{2}{4}$ $\frac{2}{2}$

shaded   white
$\frac{1}{3}$ $\frac{2}{3}$ $\frac{2}{2}$ $\frac{1}{2}$ $\frac{1}{4}$ $\frac{1}{3}$

Math: Grade 2   58   ©2006 Carson-Dellosa Publishing

Name _____

Writing the Time

An hour is sixty minutes long. It takes an hour for the BIG HAND to go around the clock. When the BIG HAND is on 12, and the little hand points to a number, that is the hour!

Directions: The **BIG HAND** is on the **12**. Color it red. The **little hand** is on the **8**. Color it blue.

The **BIG HAND** is on _____ .

The **little hand** is on _____ .

It is _____8_____ o'clock.

Name_____

Writing the Time

Directions: Color the little hour hand **red**. Fill in the blanks.

The **BIG HAND** is on _____ .

The **little hand** is on _____ .

It is _____ o'clock.

The **BIG HAND** is on _____ .

The **little hand** is on _____ .

It is _____ o'clock.

The **BIG HAND** is on _____ .

The **little hand** is on _____ .

It is _____ o'clock.

The **BIG HAND** is on _____ .

The **little hand** is on _____ .

It is _____ o'clock.

Math: Grade 2   60   ©2006 Carson-Dellosa Publishing

Name _____

Matching Digital and Face Clocks

Long ago, there were only wind-up clocks. Today, we also have electric and battery clocks. We may soon have solar clocks!

Directions: Match the digital and face clocks that show the same time.

©2006 Carson-Dellosa Publishing 61 Math: Grade 2

Name _____

Writing Time on the Half-Hour

Directions: Write the times.

_____

_____ minutes past

_____ o'clock

Half-hour later →

_____

_____ minutes past

_____ o'clock

Half-hour later →

What is your dinner time?

Directions: Circle the time you eat.

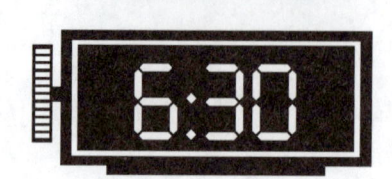

4:30   5:30   7:30
         6:30

Name _____

Counting Pennies

Directions: Count the pennies. How many cents?

Example:

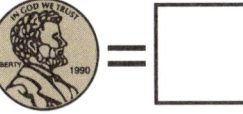

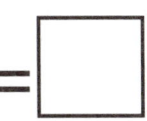

🪙 🪙 🪙 🪙 = 4¢

🪙 🪙 🪙 🪙 🪙 🪙 🪙 🪙 🪙 = ☐

🪙 🪙 🪙 🪙 🪙 = ☐

🪙 🪙 🪙 🪙 🪙 🪙 🪙 🪙 🪙 🪙 = ☐

🪙 🪙 🪙 = ☐

🪙 🪙 🪙 🪙 🪙 🪙 = ☐

🪙 🪙 🪙 🪙 🪙 🪙 🪙 = ☐

🪙 🪙 = ☐

🪙 🪙 🪙 🪙 🪙 🪙 🪙 🪙 🪙 🪙 🪙 = ☐

Name _____

Nickels: Counting by Fives

Directions: Count the nickels by 5s. Write the amount.

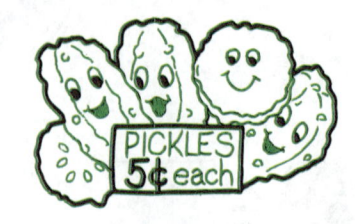

Example:

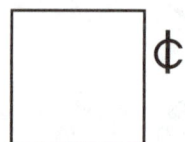

5 cents = 1 nickel

☐ 15 ¢

☐ ¢

Count 5 , 10 , 15 .

Count ___ , ___ .

☐ ¢

☐ ¢

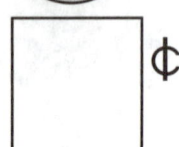

Count ___ , ___ , ___ .

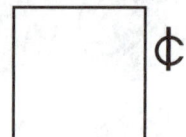

Count ___ , ___ , ___ , ___ .

☐ ¢

☐ ¢

Count ___ , ___ , ___ , ___ .

Count ___ , ___ , ___ , ___ , ___ .

Math: Grade 2   64   ©2006 Carson-Dellosa Publishing

Dimes: Counting by Tens

Directions: Count by 10s. Write the number. Circle the group with more.

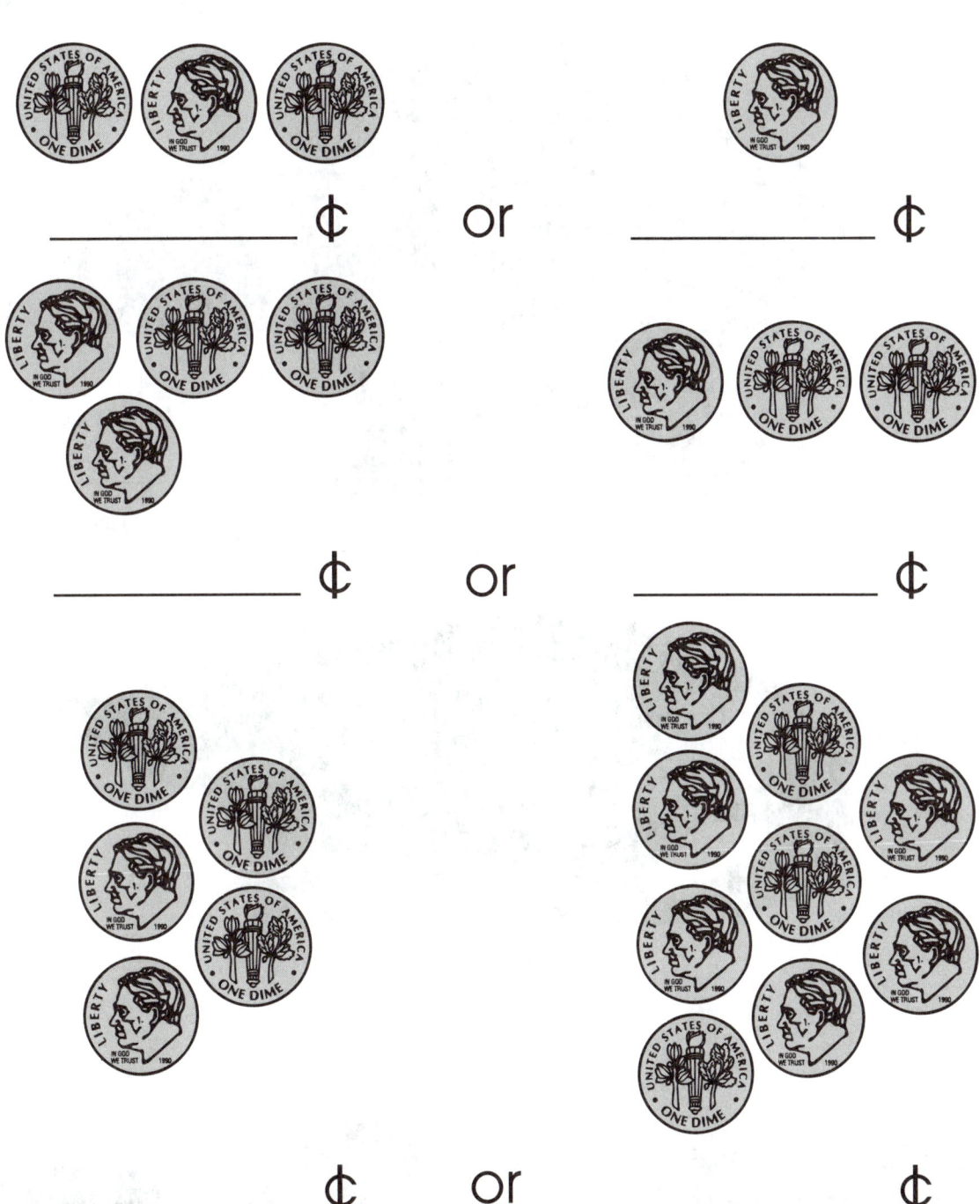

_____ ¢   or   _____ ¢

_____ ¢   or   _____ ¢

_____ ¢   or   _____ ¢

Name_____

Counting With Dimes, Nickels, and Pennies

Directions: Count the money. Start with the dime. Write the amount.

1.  _____ ¢

2.  _____ ¢

3. Circle the answer.
   Who has more money?

Math: Grade 2   ©2006 Carson-Dellosa Publishing

Name _____

Counting With Quarters, Dimes, Nickels, and Pennies

Directions: Match the money with the amount.

nickel, nickel, nickel   **35 ¢**

dime, dime, penny   **36 ¢**

quarter, penny, penny   **40 ¢**

quarter, nickel, nickel   **27 ¢**

dime, dime, dime, dime   **15 ¢**

nickel, penny, penny, penny   **21 ¢**

quarter, dime, penny   **8 ¢**

©2006 Carson-Dellosa Publishing   67   Math: Grade 2

Name _____

Making Exact Amounts of Money: Two Ways to Pay

Directions: Find two ways to pay. Show what coins you use.

27¢

1.

_____ quarters
_____ dimes
_____ nickels
_____ pennies

2.

_____ quarters
_____ dimes
_____ nickels
_____ pennies

32¢

3.

_____ quarters
_____ dimes
_____ nickels
_____ pennies

4.

_____ quarters
_____ dimes
_____ nickels
_____ pennies

Math: Grade 2   ©2006 Carson-Dellosa Publishing

Making Exact Amounts of Money: How Much More?

Directions: Count the coins. Find out how much more money you need to pay the exact amount.

How much money do you have? _____ ¢

How much more money do you need? _____ ¢

How much money do you have? _____ ¢

How much more money do you need? _____ ¢

Solve this puzzle.

How much more money does Monkey need?

_____ ¢

I have 1 quarter and 4 dimes. I need one more coin to pay for the banana-van.

Answer Key

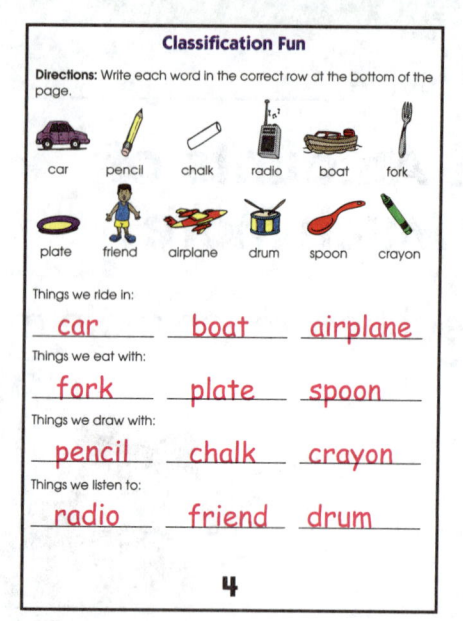

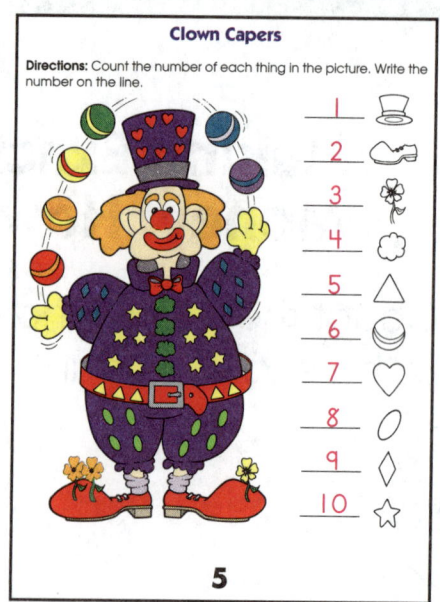

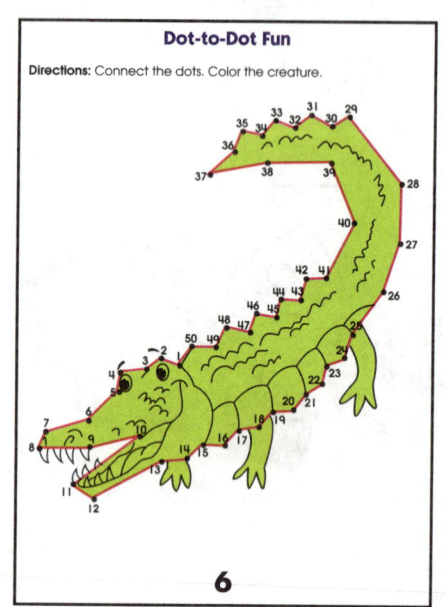

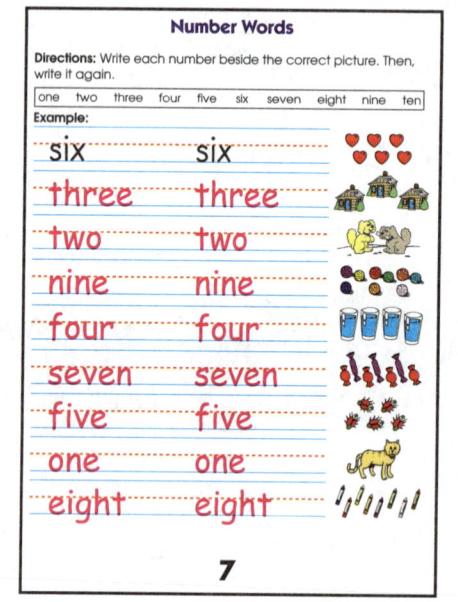

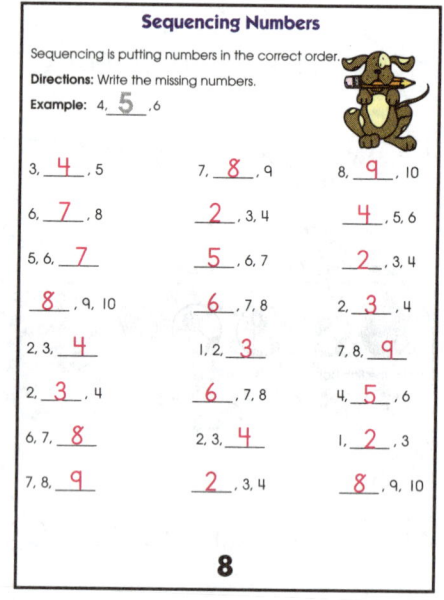

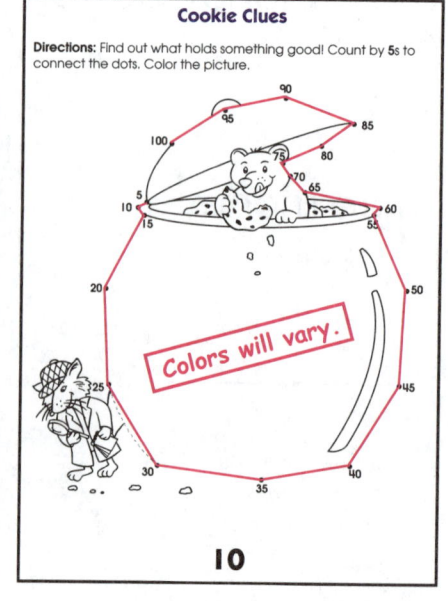

Classification Fun
Directions: Write each word in the correct row at the bottom of the page.

Things we ride in: car, boat, airplane
Things we eat with: fork, plate, spoon
Things we draw with: pencil, chalk, crayon
Things we listen to: radio, friend, drum

4

Clown Capers
Directions: Count the number of each thing in the picture. Write the number on the line.

1, 2, 3, 4, 5, 6, 7, 8, 9, 10

5

Dot-to-Dot Fun
Directions: Connect the dots. Color the creature.

6

Number Words
Directions: Write each number beside the correct picture. Then, write it again.

one two three four five six seven eight nine ten

Example: six — six
three — three
two — two
nine — nine
four — four
seven — seven
five — five
one — one
eight — eight

7

Sequencing Numbers
Sequencing is putting numbers in the correct order.
Directions: Write the missing numbers.
Example: 4, **5**, 6

3, **4**, 5   7, **8**, 9   8, **9**, 10
6, **7**, 8   **2**, 3, 4   **4**, 5, 6
5, 6, **7**   **5**, 6, 7   **2**, 3, 4
8, 9, 10   **6**, 7, 8   2, **3**, 4
2, 3, **4**   1, 2, **3**   7, 8, **9**
2, **3**, 4   **6**, 7, 8   4, **5**, 6
6, 7, **8**   2, 3, **4**   1, **2**, 3
7, 8, **9**   **2**, 3, 4   **8**, 9, 10

8

Two for the Pool
Directions: Count by **2s**. Write the numbers to **30** in the water drops. Begin at the top of the slide and go down.

2, 4, 6, 8, 10, 12, 14, 16, 18, 20, 22, 24, 26, 28, 30

9

Cookie Clues
Directions: Find out what holds something good! Count by 5s to connect the dots. Color the picture.

Colors will vary.

10

Math: Grade 2   70   ©2006 Carson-Dellosa Publishing

Desert Trek

Directions: Count by 10s. Color each canteen with a 10 to lead the camel to the watering hole.

(Canteens colored red: 10, 20, 30, 40, 50, 60, 70, 80, 90, 100; uncolored: 25, 35, 15, 5, 65, 85, 75)

"Mouth" Math

Directions: Write < or > in each circle. Make sure the "mouth" is open toward the greater number!

36 < 49   35 < 53
20 > 18   74 > 21
53 < 76   68 < 80
29 > 26   45 > 19
90 > 89   70 > 67

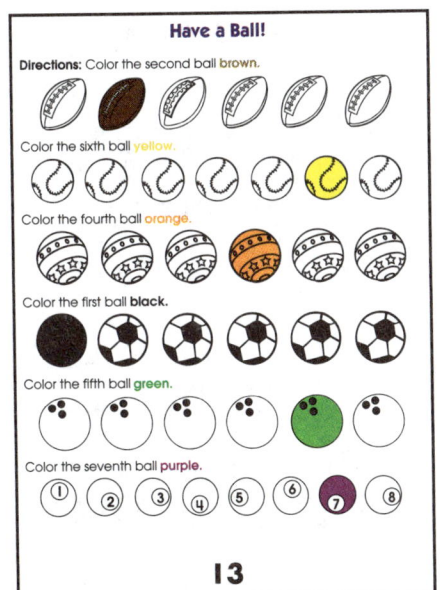

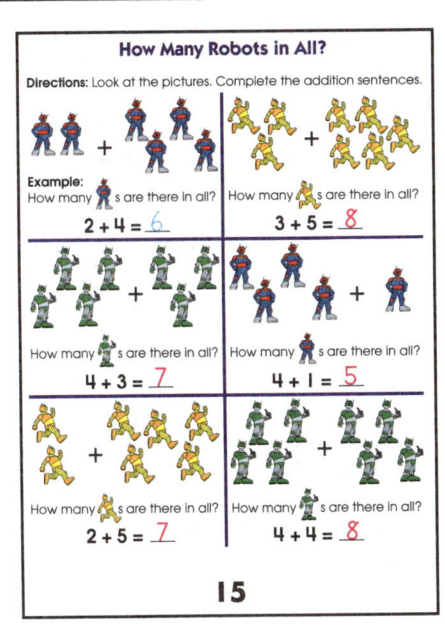

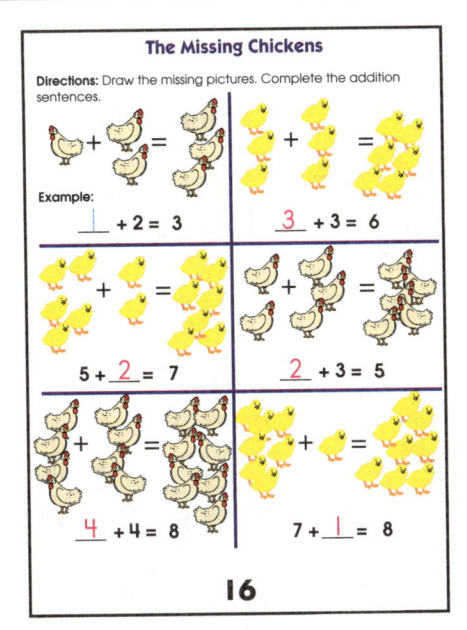

Have a Ball!

Directions: Color the second ball brown.
Color the sixth ball yellow.
Color the fourth ball orange.
Color the first ball black.
Color the fifth ball green.
Color the seventh ball purple.

Which Place in the Race?

Directions: Write the correct word to tell each runner's place in the race.

fifth
first
fourth
third
seventh
second
sixth

How Many Robots in All?

Directions: Look at the pictures. Complete the addition sentences.

Example:
2 + 4 = 6   3 + 5 = 8
4 + 3 = 7   4 + 1 = 5
2 + 5 = 7   4 + 4 = 8

The Missing Chickens

Directions: Draw the missing pictures. Complete the addition sentences.

Example: 1 + 2 = 3   3 + 3 = 6
5 + 2 = 7   2 + 3 = 5
4 + 4 = 8   7 + 1 = 8

Counting Up

Directions: Count up to get the sum. Write the missing addend in each blank.

3 + 3 = 6   8 + 1 = 9
4 + 1 = 5   4 + 2 = 6
7 + 2 = 9   6 + 0 = 6
2 + 2 = 4   5 + 2 = 7
3 + 5 = 8   4 + 3 = 7
5 + 0 = 5   9 + 1 = 10
8 + 2 = 10   5 + 3 = 8
7 + 1 = 8   7 + 3 = 10
6 + 3 = 9   6 + 2 = 8

Coloring by Number

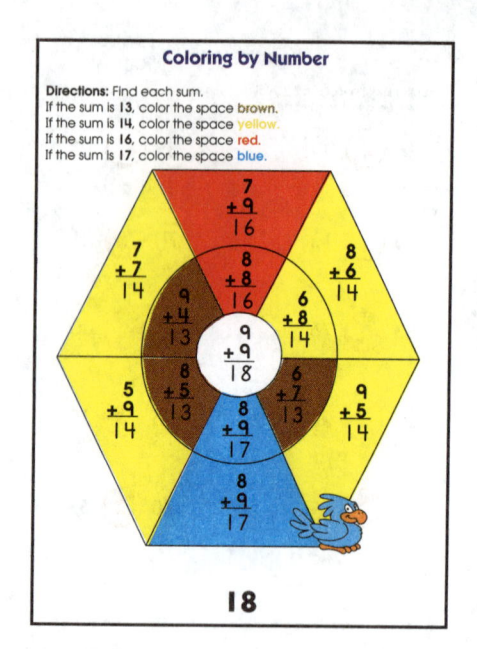

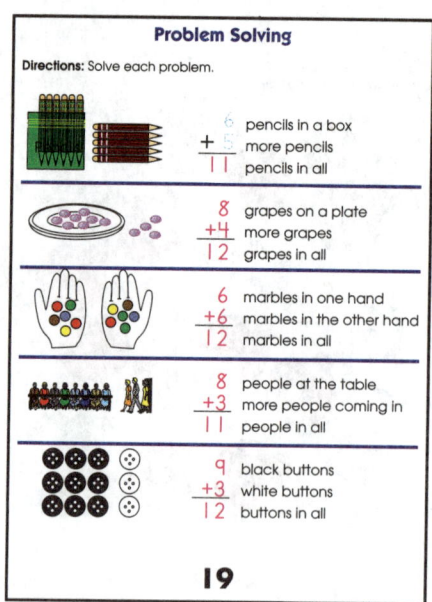

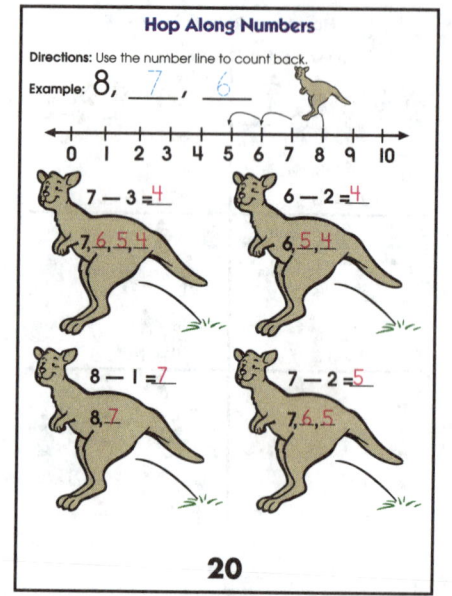

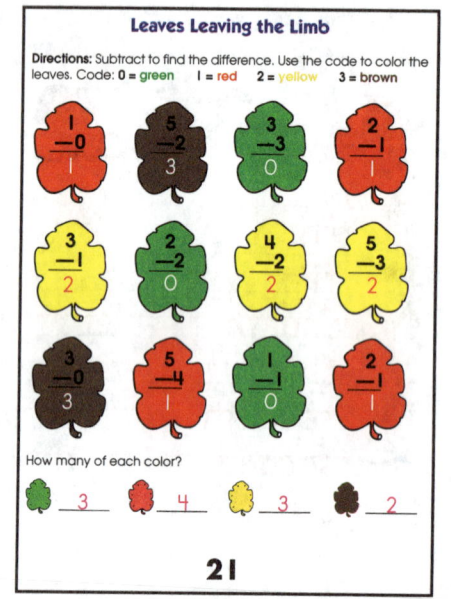

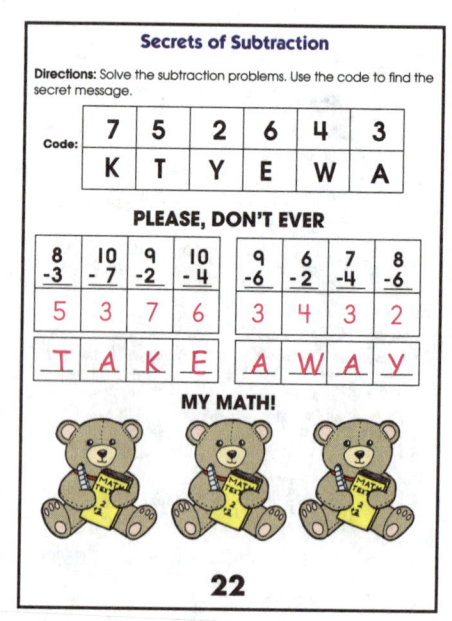

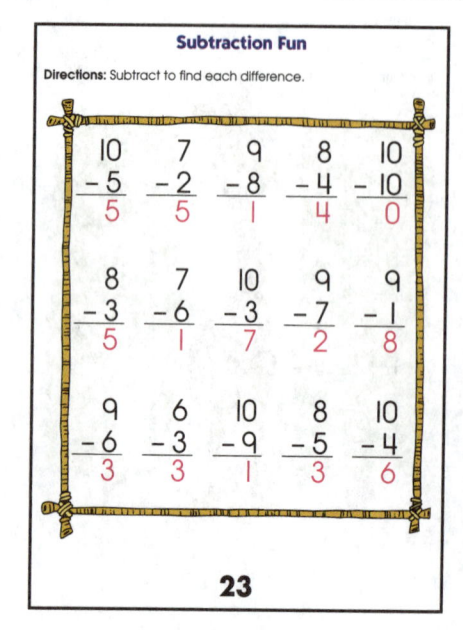

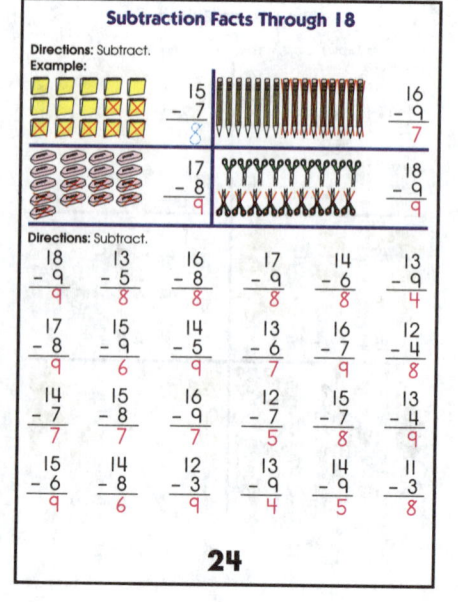

Directions: Find each sum.
If the sum is 13, color the space brown.
If the sum is 14, color the space yellow.
If the sum is 16, color the space red.
If the sum is 17, color the space blue.

7 + 9 = 16
7 + 7 = 14
8 + 6 = 14
9 + 4 = 13
8 + 8 = 16
6 + 8 = 14
9 + 9 = 18
5 + 9 = 14
8 + 5 = 13
6 + 7 = 13
9 + 5 = 14
8 + 9 = 17

18

Problem Solving

Directions: Solve each problem.

6 pencils in a box
+ 5 more pencils
11 pencils in all

8 grapes on a plate
+ 4 more grapes
12 grapes in all

6 marbles in one hand
+ 6 marbles in the other hand
12 marbles in all

8 people at the table
+ 3 more people coming in
11 people in all

9 black buttons
+ 3 white buttons
12 buttons in all

19

Hop Along Numbers

Directions: Use the number line to count back.

Example: 8, _7_, _6_

7 − 3 = 4   7, 6, 5, 4
6 − 2 = 4   6, 5, 4
8 − 1 = 7   8, 7
7 − 2 = 5   7, 6, 5

20

Leaves Leaving the Limb

Directions: Subtract to find the difference. Use the code to color the leaves. Code: 0 = green 1 = red 2 = yellow 3 = brown

1 − 0 = 1
5 − 2 = 3
3 − 3 = 0
2 − 1 = 1
3 − 1 = 2
2 − 2 = 0
4 − 2 = 2
5 − 3 = 2
3 − 0 = 3
5 − 4 = 1
1 − 1 = 0
2 − 1 = 1

How many of each color?
green _3_   red _4_   yellow _3_   brown _2_

21

Secrets of Subtraction

Directions: Solve the subtraction problems. Use the code to find the secret message.

Code:
| 7 | 5 | 2 | 6 | 4 | 3 |
| K | T | Y | E | W | A |

PLEASE, DON'T EVER

8 − 3 = 5
10 − 7 = 3
9 − 2 = 7
10 − 4 = 6
9 − 6 = 3
6 − 2 = 4
7 − 4 = 3
8 − 6 = 2

T A K E   A W A Y

MY MATH!

22

Subtraction Fun

Directions: Subtract to find each difference.

10 − 5 = 5
7 − 2 = 5
9 − 8 = 1
8 − 4 = 4
10 − 10 = 0

8 − 3 = 5
7 − 6 = 1
10 − 3 = 7
9 − 7 = 2
9 − 1 = 8

9 − 6 = 3
6 − 3 = 3
10 − 9 = 1
8 − 5 = 3
10 − 4 = 6

23

Subtraction Facts Through 18

Directions: Subtract.
Example:

15 − 7 = 8
16 − 9 = 7
17 − 8 = 9
18 − 9 = 9

Directions: Subtract.

18 − 9 = 9
13 − 5 = 8
16 − 8 = 8
17 − 9 = 8
14 − 6 = 8
13 − 9 = 4

17 − 8 = 9
15 − 9 = 6
14 − 5 = 9
13 − 6 = 7
16 − 7 = 9
12 − 4 = 8

14 − 7 = 7
15 − 8 = 7
16 − 9 = 7
12 − 7 = 5
15 − 7 = 8
13 − 4 = 9

15 − 6 = 9
14 − 8 = 6
12 − 3 = 9
13 − 9 = 4
14 − 9 = 5
11 − 3 = 8

24

Math: Grade 2   72   ©2006 Carson-Dellosa Publishing

"Grrreat" Picture

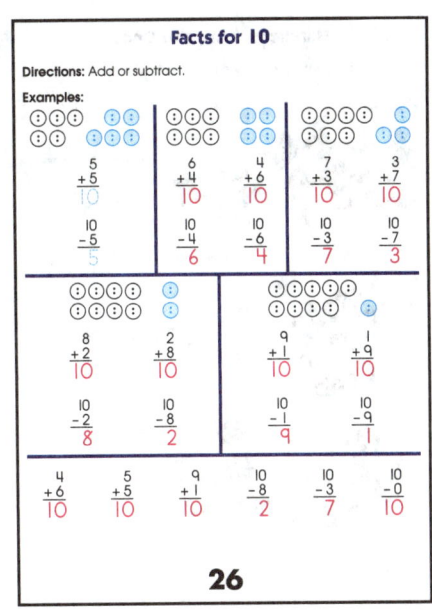

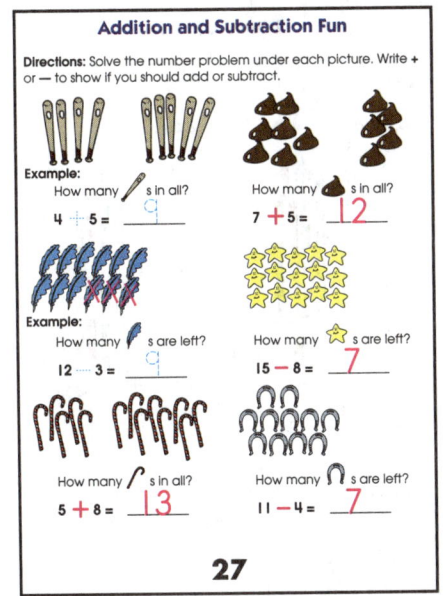

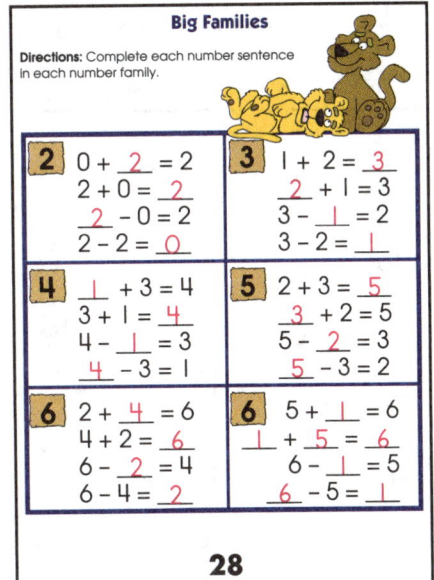

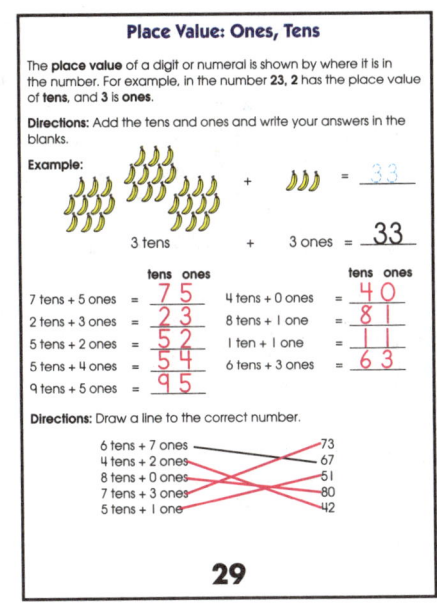

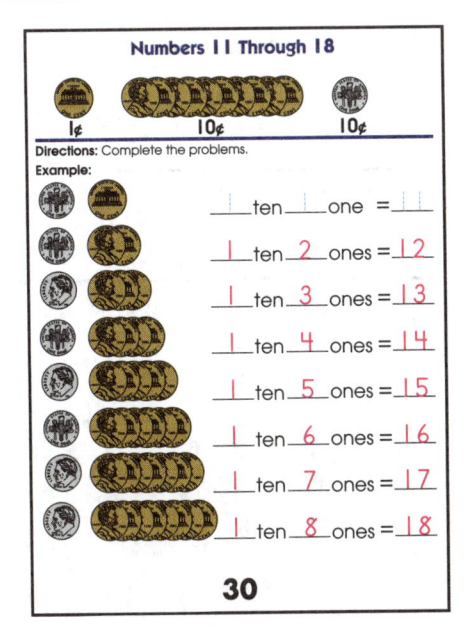

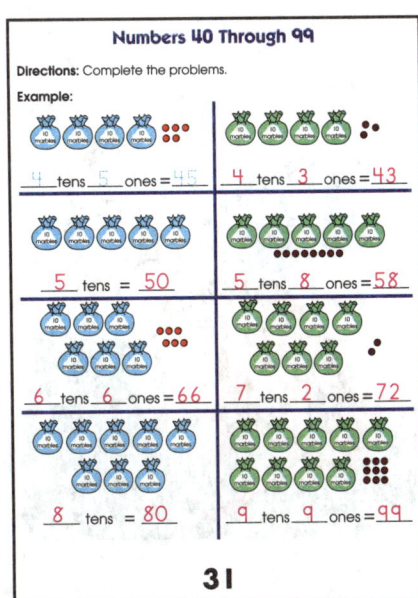

Directions: Subtract. Write the answer in the space. Then, color the spaces according to the answers.

1 = white 2 = purple 3 = black 4 = green 5 = yellow
6 = blue 7 = pink 8 = gray 9 = orange 10 = red

25

Facts for 10

Directions: Add or subtract.

Examples:

$5 + 5 = 10$ $6 + 4 = 10$ $4 + 6 = 10$ $7 + 3 = 10$ $3 + 7 = 10$

$10 - 5 = 5$ $10 - 4 = 6$ $10 - 6 = 4$ $10 - 3 = 7$ $10 - 7 = 3$

$8 + 2 = 10$ $2 + 8 = 10$ $9 + 1 = 10$ $1 + 9 = 10$

$10 - 2 = 8$ $10 - 8 = 2$ $10 - 1 = 9$ $10 - 9 = 1$

$4 + 6 = 10$ $5 + 5 = 10$ $9 + 1 = 10$ $10 - 8 = 2$ $10 - 3 = 7$ $10 - 0 = 10$

26

Addition and Subtraction Fun

Directions: Solve the number problem under each picture. Write + or − to show if you should add or subtract.

Example:
How many 🖊s in all?
$4 + 5 = 9$

How many 🍫s in all?
$7 + 5 = 12$

Example:
How many 🪶s are left?
$12 - 3 = 9$

How many ⭐s are left?
$15 - 8 = 7$

How many 🦯s in all?
$5 + 8 = 13$

How many ⌒s are left?
$11 - 4 = 7$

27

Big Families

Directions: Complete each number sentence in each number family.

2
$0 + 2 = 2$
$2 + 0 = 2$
$2 - 0 = 2$
$2 - 2 = 0$

3
$1 + 2 = 3$
$2 + 1 = 3$
$3 - 1 = 2$
$3 - 2 = 1$

4
$1 + 3 = 4$
$3 + 1 = 4$
$4 - 1 = 3$
$4 - 3 = 1$

5
$2 + 3 = 5$
$3 + 2 = 5$
$5 - 2 = 3$
$5 - 3 = 2$

6
$2 + 4 = 6$
$4 + 2 = 6$
$6 - 2 = 4$
$6 - 4 = 2$

6
$5 + 1 = 6$
$1 + 5 = 6$
$6 - 1 = 5$
$6 - 5 = 1$

28

Place Value: Ones, Tens

The **place value** of a digit or numeral is shown by where it is in the number. For example, in the number **23**, **2** has the place value of **tens**, and **3** is **ones**.

Directions: Add the tens and ones and write your answers in the blanks.

Example:
3 tens + 3 ones = 33

	tens ones		tens ones
7 tens + 5 ones =	75	4 tens + 0 ones =	40
2 tens + 3 ones =	23	8 tens + 1 one =	81
5 tens + 2 ones =	52	1 ten + 1 one =	11
5 tens + 4 ones =	54	6 tens + 3 ones =	63
9 tens + 5 ones =	95		

Directions: Draw a line to the correct number.

6 tens + 7 ones — 73
4 tens + 2 ones — 67
8 tens + 0 ones — 51
7 tens + 3 ones — 80
5 tens + 1 one — 42

29

Numbers 11 Through 18

1¢   10¢   10¢

Directions: Complete the problems.

Example:
1 ten 1 one = 11
1 ten 2 ones = 12
1 ten 3 ones = 13
1 ten 4 ones = 14
1 ten 5 ones = 15
1 ten 6 ones = 16
1 ten 7 ones = 17
1 ten 8 ones = 18

30

Numbers 40 Through 99

Directions: Complete the problems.

Example:
4 tens 5 ones = 45   4 tens 3 ones = 43

5 tens = 50   5 tens 8 ones = 58

6 tens 6 ones = 66   7 tens 2 ones = 72

8 tens = 80   9 tens 9 ones = 99

31

32. Hundreds, Tens, and Ones

Directions: Count the groups of crayons. Write the number of hundreds, tens, and ones.

Example: 1 Hundred + 1 Ten + 3 Ones = 1 1 3

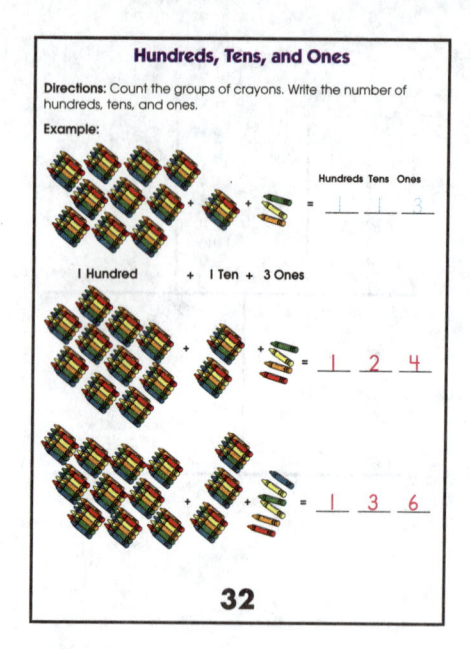

1 2 4

1 3 6

33. Count 'Em Up!

Directions: Look at the example. Then, write the missing numbers in the blanks.

Example: 2 hundreds + 3 tens + 6 ones = 236

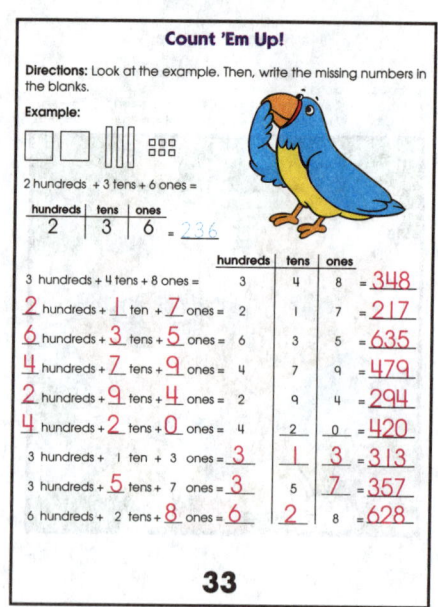

	hundreds	tens	ones	
3 hundreds + 4 tens + 8 ones =	3	4	8	348
2 hundreds + 1 ten + 7 ones =	2	1	7	217
6 hundreds + 3 tens + 5 ones =	6	3	5	635
4 hundreds + 7 tens + 9 ones =	4	7	9	479
2 hundreds + 9 tens + 4 ones =	2	9	4	294
4 hundreds + 2 tens + 0 ones =	4	2	0	420
3 hundreds + 1 ten + 3 ones =	3	1	3	313
3 hundreds + 5 tens + 7 ones =	3	5	7	357
6 hundreds + 2 tens + 8 ones =	6	2	8	628

34. Place Value: Thousands

Directions: Study the example. Write the missing numbers.

Example: 1,000 / 100 / 10 / 1
1,000 / / 10 / 1
/ / 10 /

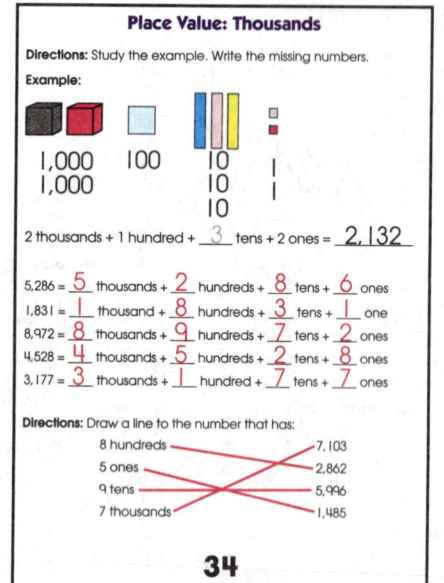

2 thousands + 1 hundred + 3 tens + 2 ones = 2,132

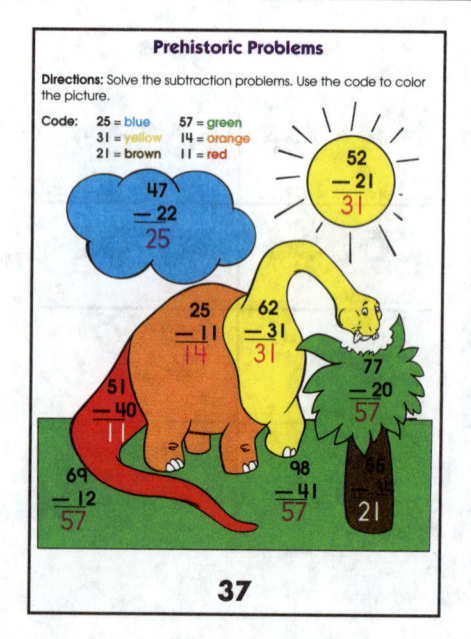

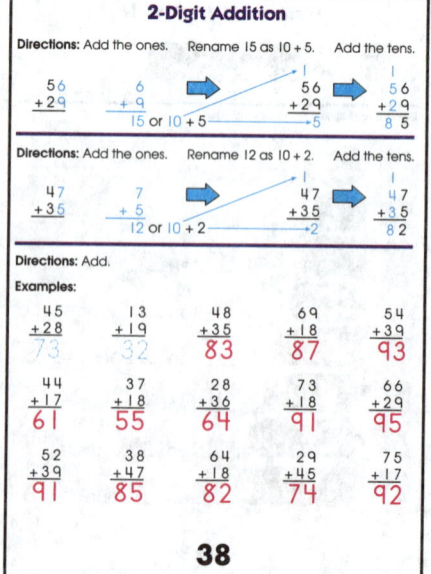

5,286 = 5 thousands + 2 hundreds + 8 tens + 6 ones
1,831 = 1 thousand + 8 hundreds + 3 tens + 1 one
8,972 = 8 thousands + 9 hundreds + 7 tens + 2 ones
4,528 = 4 thousands + 5 hundreds + 2 tens + 8 ones
3,177 = 3 thousands + 1 hundred + 7 tens + 7 ones

Directions: Draw a line to the number that has:

8 hundreds — 7,103
5 ones — 2,862
9 tens — 5,996
7 thousands — 1,485

35. Adding Tens

```
 3 tens     30       6 tens     60
+4 tens    +40      +2 tens    +20
 7 tens     70       8 tens     80
```

Directions: Add.

```
 2 tens    20        6 tens    60
+4 tens   +40       +2 tens   +20
 6 tens    60        8 tens    80

 20   10   40   30   50
+20  +50  +20  +40  +30
 40   60   60   70   80

 30   60   20   70   10
+20  +10  +50  +10  +10
 50   70   70   80   20

 10   40   80   60   20
+20  +40  +10  +30  +60
 30   80   90   90   80

 70   40   30   50   30
+20  +10  +10  +40  +30
 90   50   40   90   60
```

36. 2-Digit Addition

Directions: Study the example. Follow the steps to add.

Example: 33 + 41

Step 1: Add the ones. Step 2: Add the tens.

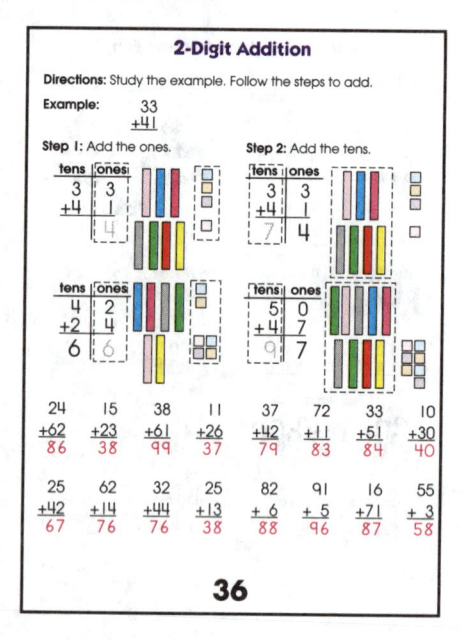

```
tens ones       tens ones
  3    3          3    3
 +4    1         +4    1
       4          7    4

  4    2          5    0
 +2    4         +4    7
  6    6          9    7

 24   15   38   11   37   72   33   10
+62  +23  +61  +26  +42  +11  +51  +30
 86   38   99   37   79   83   84   40

 25   62   32   25   82   91   16   55
+42  +14  +44  +13  + 6  + 5  +71  + 3
 67   76   76   38   88   96   87   58
```

37. Prehistoric Problems

Directions: Solve the subtraction problems. Use the code to color the picture.

Code: 25 = blue   57 = green
      31 = yellow 14 = orange
      21 = brown   11 = red

```
 47     52     25     62     77
-22    -21    -11    -31    -20
 25     31     14     31     57

 51     69     98     66
-40    -12    -41    -41
 11     57     57     21
```

38. 2-Digit Addition

Directions: Add the ones. Rename 15 as 10 + 5. Add the tens.

```
 56      6         1        1
+29     +9         56       56
        15 or 10+5 +29      +29
                    5       85
```

Directions: Add the ones. Rename 12 as 10 + 2. Add the tens.

```
 47      7         1        1
+35     +5         47       47
        12 or 10+2 +35      +35
                    2       82
```

Directions: Add.

Examples:
```
 45   13   48   69   54
+28  +19  +35  +18  +39
 73   32   83   87   93

 44   37   28   73   66
+17  +18  +36  +18  +29
 61   55   64   91   95

 52   38   64   29   75
+39  +47  +18  +45  +17
 91   85   82   74   92
```

Math: Grade 2   74   ©2006 Carson-Dellosa Publishing

2-Digit Subtraction: Regrouping

Subtraction is "taking away" or subtracting one number from another to find the difference. Regrouping is using **one ten** to form **ten ones**, **one 100** to form **ten tens**, and so on.

Directions: Study the examples. Follow the steps to subtract.

Example: 37
−19

Step 1: Regroup.
Step 2: Subtract the ones.
Step 3: Subtract the tens.

28	46	12	30	52	47	21	45
−19	−18	−8	−12	−25	−35	−13	−25
9	28	4	18	27	12	8	20

39

Addition and Subtraction Review

Directions: Add.

4	8	9	7	5	6
+9	+6	+8	+6	+7	+5
13	14	17	13	12	11

9	5	7	9	8	7
+6	+8	+4	+9	+7	+9
15	13	11	18	15	16

30	20	45	52	60	83
+40	+30	+23	+23	+25	+15
70	50	68	75	85	98

Directions: Subtract.

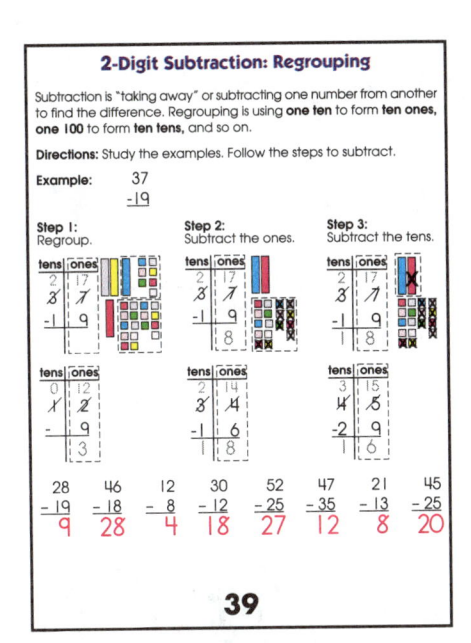

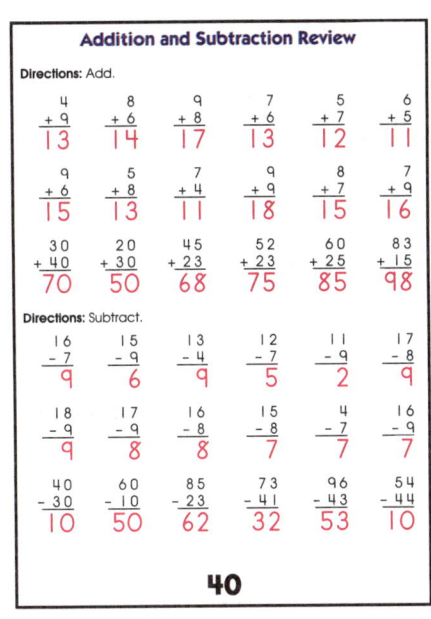

16	15	13	12	11	17
−7	−9	−4	−7	−9	−8
9	6	9	5	2	9

18	17	16	15	4	16
−9	−9	−8	−8	−7	−9
9	8	8	7	7	7

40	60	85	73	96	54
−30	−10	−23	−41	−43	−44
10	50	62	32	53	10

40

Adding Hundreds

Examples:
5 hundreds   500   4 hundreds   400
+ 3 hundreds   + 300   + 5 hundreds   + 500
8 hundreds   800   9 hundreds   900

Directions: Add.

3 hundreds   300   6 hundreds   600
+ 1 hundreds   + 100   + 2 hundreds   + 200
4 hundreds   400   8 hundreds   800

200	100	600	400
+200	+700	+300	+500
400	800	900	900

300	800	400	700
+400	+100	+400	+200
700	900	800	900

500	100	500	300
+100	+600	+200	+200
600	700	700	500

300	400	300	200
+300	+200	+500	+100
600	600	800	300

41

3-Digit Addition

245 → 245 → 245
+253   +253   +253
   8   98   498

Directions: Add.

Example:
745   623
+ 23   +156
 768   779

Add the ones.
Add the tens.
Add the hundreds.

415	566	373	160
+342	+33	+221	+334
757	599	594	494

835	642	287	723
+42	+251	+412	+45
877	893	699	768

133	454	314	654
+522	+324	+602	+235
655	778	916	889

42

Subtracting Hundreds

8 hundreds   800   6 hundreds   600
− 3 hundreds   − 300   − 2 hundreds   − 200
5 hundreds   500   4 hundreds   400

Directions: Subtract.

Example:
9 hundreds   900   3 hundreds   300
− 7 hundreds   − 700   − 1 hundreds   − 100
2 hundreds   200   2 hundreds   200

700	500	900	800
−300	−400	−400	−500
400	100	500	300

600	300	500	400
−500	−200	−100	−200
100	100	400	200

900	800	600	500
−100	−400	−200	−300
800	400	400	200

400	700	800	900
−100	−600	−200	−600
300	100	600	300

43

Problem Solving

Directions: Solve each problem.

Example:
The grocery store buys 568 cans of beans.
It sells 345 cans of beans.
How many cans of beans are left?
568 − 345 = 223

The cooler holds 732 gallons of milk.
It has 412 gallons of milk in it.
How many more gallons of milk will it take to fill the cooler?
732 − 412 = 320

Ann does 635 push-ups.
Carl does 421 push-ups.
How many more push-ups does Ann do?
635 − 421 = 214

Kurt has 386 pennies.
Neal has 32 pennies.
How many more pennies does Kurt have?
386 − 32 = 354

It takes 874 nails to build a tree house.
Jillian has 532 nails.
How many more nails does she need?
874 − 532 = 342

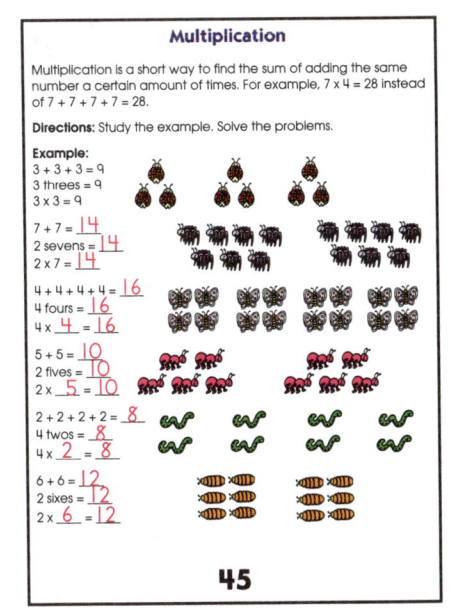

44

Multiplication

Multiplication is a short way to find the sum of adding the same number a certain amount of times. For example, 7 × 4 = 28 instead of 7 + 7 + 7 + 7 = 28.

Directions: Study the example. Solve the problems.

Example:
3 + 3 + 3 = 9
3 threes = 9
3 × 3 = 9

7 + 7 = 14
2 sevens = 14
2 × 7 = 14

4 + 4 + 4 + 4 = 16
4 fours = 16
4 × 4 = 16

5 + 5 = 10
2 fives = 10
2 × 5 = 10

2 + 2 + 2 + 2 = 8
4 twos = 8
4 × 2 = 8

6 + 6 = 12
2 sixes = 12
2 × 6 = 12

45

Multiplication

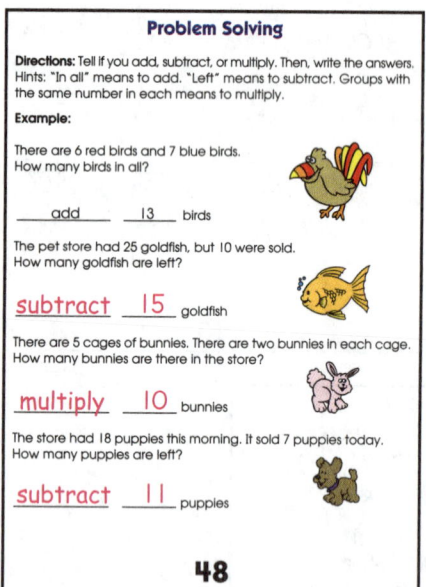

Directions: Solve the problems.

9 + 9 = 18   7 + 7 = 14
2 nines = 18   2 sevens = 14
2 x 9 = 18   2 x 7 = 14

Multiplication saves time. It's faster than addition!

4 + 4 + 4 + 4 = 16   8 + 8 + 8 + 8 + 8 = 40
4 fours = 16   5 eights = 40
4 x 4 = 16   5 x 8 = 40

5 + 5 + 5 = 15   9 + 9 = 18   6 + 6 + 6 = 18
3 fives = 15   2 nines = 18   3 sixes = 18
3 x 5 = 15   2 x 9 = 18   3 x 6 = 18

3 + 3 = 6   7 + 7 + 7 + 7 = 28   2 + 2 = 4
2 threes = 6   4 sevens = 28   2 twos = 4
2 x 3 = 6   4 x 7 = 28   2 x 2 = 4

46

Multiplication

Directions: Use the code to color the fish.

If the answer is:
- 6, color it red.
- 12, color it orange.
- 16, color it blue.
- 27, color it brown.
- 8, color it yellow.
- 15, color it green.
- 18, color it purple.

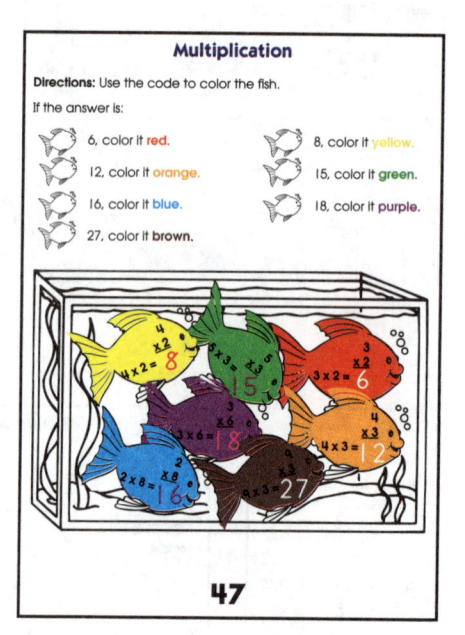

47

Problem Solving

Directions: Tell if you add, subtract, or multiply. Then, write the answers. Hints: "In all" means to add. "Left" means to subtract. Groups with the same number in each means to multiply.

Example:

There are 6 red birds and 7 blue birds. How many birds in all?

____add____   __13__ birds

The pet store had 25 goldfish, but 10 were sold. How many goldfish are left?

__subtract__ __15__ goldfish

There are 5 cages of bunnies. There are two bunnies in each cage. How many bunnies are there in the store?

__multiply__ __10__ bunnies

The store had 18 puppies this morning. It sold 7 puppies today. How many puppies are left?

__subtract__ __11__ puppies

48

Geometry

Geometry is mathematics that has to do with lines and shapes.

Directions: Color the shapes.

Color the triangles blue.
Color the circles red.
Color the squares green.
Color the rectangles pink.

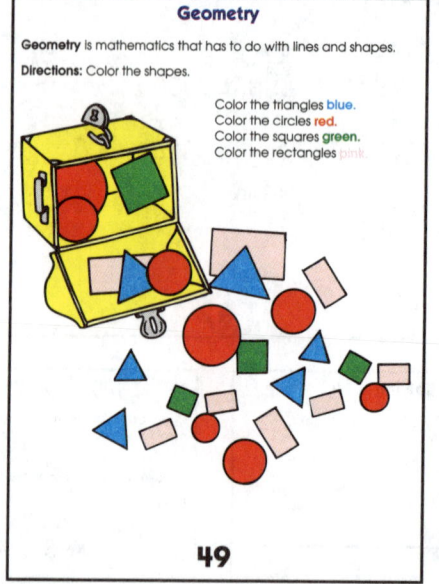

49

Shapes

Directions: Look at the grid below. All the shapes have straight sides, like a square.

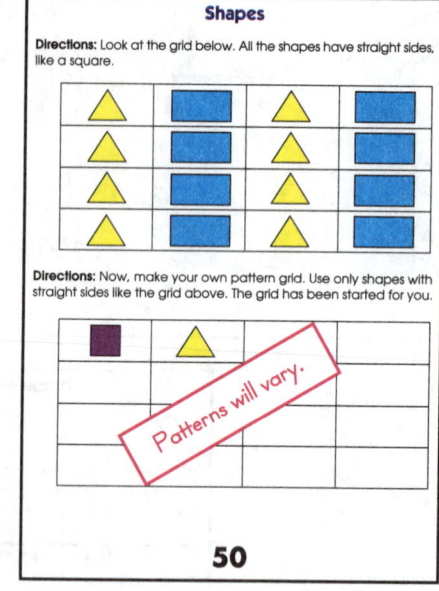

Directions: Now, make your own pattern grid. Use only shapes with straight sides like the grid above. The grid has been started for you.

Patterns will vary.

50

Math: Grade 2   76   ©2006 Carson-Dellosa Publishing

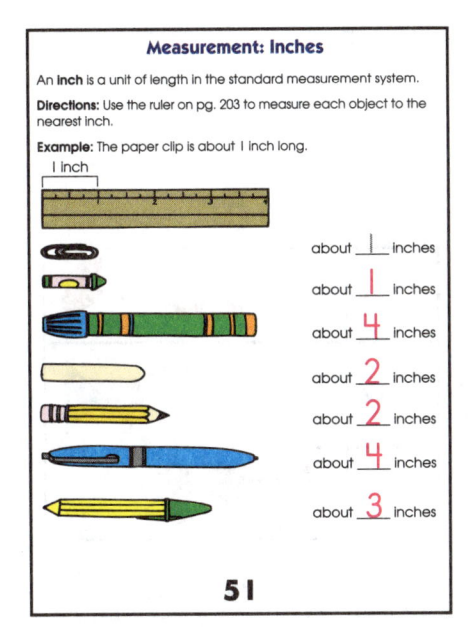

Measurement: Inches

An **inch** is a unit of length in the standard measurement system.

Directions: Use the ruler on pg. 203 to measure each object to the nearest inch.

Example: The paper clip is about 1 inch long.

about **1** inches
about **1** inches
about **4** inches
about **2** inches
about **2** inches
about **4** inches
about **3** inches

51

Measuring in Centimeters

Directions: Use a centimeter ruler to find the height or the length of the objects below. Write the answer in each blank.

Example: **14** cm

12 cm
20 cm
6 cm
6 cm
3 cm

52

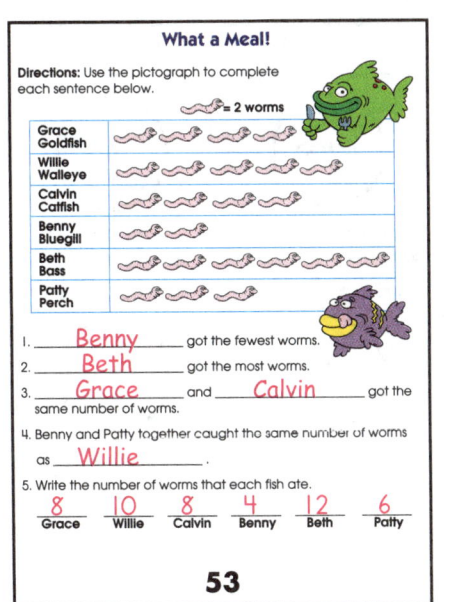

What a Meal!

Directions: Use the pictograph to complete each sentence below.

= 2 worms

1. **Benny** got the fewest worms.
2. **Beth** got the most worms.
3. **Grace** and **Calvin** got the same number of worms.
4. Benny and Patty together caught the same number of worms as **Willie**.
5. Write the number of worms that each fish ate.

8 Grace   **10** Willie   **8** Calvin   **4** Benny   **12** Beth   **6** Patty

53

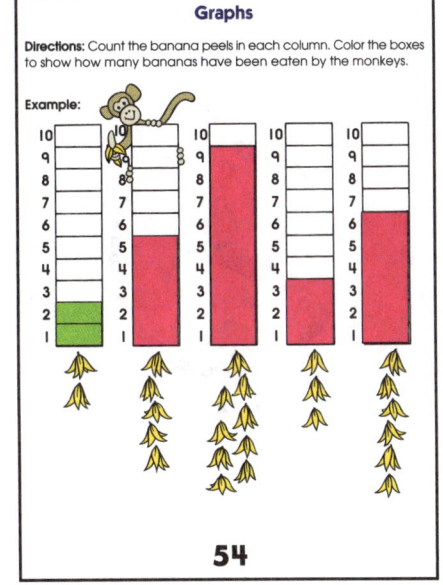

Graphs

Directions: Count the banana peels in each column. Color the boxes to show how many bananas have been eaten by the monkeys.

Example:

54

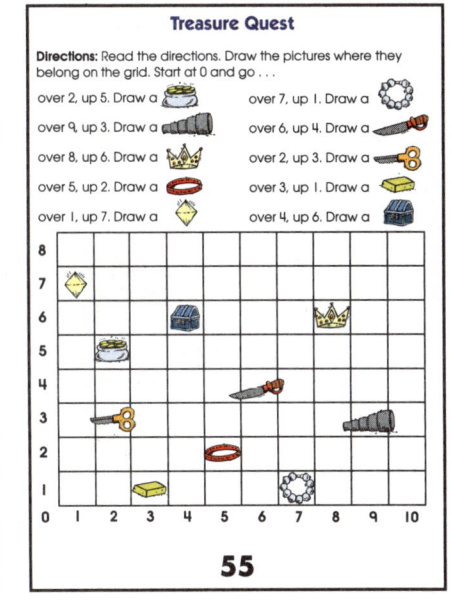

Treasure Quest

Directions: Read the directions. Draw the pictures where they belong on the grid. Start at 0 and go . . .

over 2, up 5. Draw a 🥣
over 9, up 3. Draw a 🔭
over 8, up 6. Draw a 👑
over 5, up 2. Draw a ⭕
over 1, up 7. Draw a 💎

over 7, up 1. Draw a 💍
over 6, up 4. Draw a 🗡
over 2, up 3. Draw a ✂
over 3, up 1. Draw a 🧱
over 4, up 6. Draw a 📦

55

77

Math: Grade 2

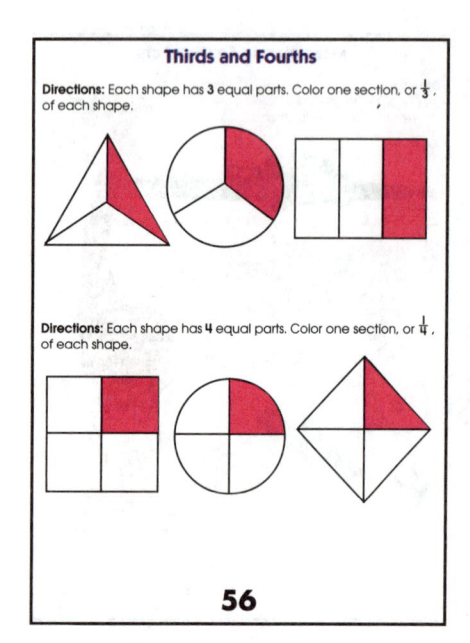

Thirds and Fourths

Directions: Each shape has **3** equal parts. Color one section, or $\frac{1}{3}$, of each shape.

Directions: Each shape has **4** equal parts. Color one section, or $\frac{1}{4}$, of each shape.

56

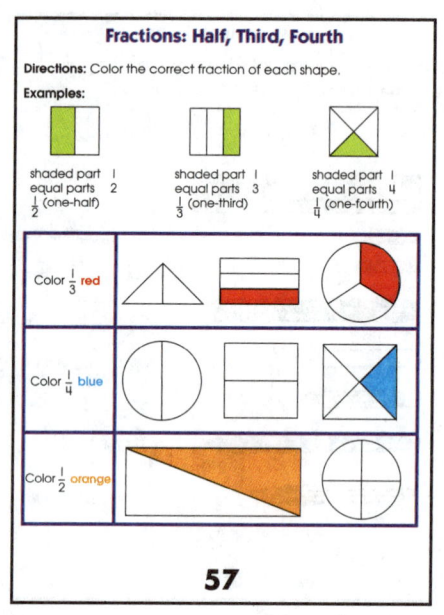

Fractions: Half, Third, Fourth

Directions: Color the correct fraction of each shape.

Examples:

shaded part 1
equal parts 2
$\frac{1}{2}$ (one-half)

shaded part 1
equal parts 3
$\frac{1}{3}$ (one-third)

shaded part 1
equal parts 4
$\frac{1}{4}$ (one-fourth)

Color $\frac{1}{3}$ red

Color $\frac{1}{4}$ blue

Color $\frac{1}{2}$ orange

57

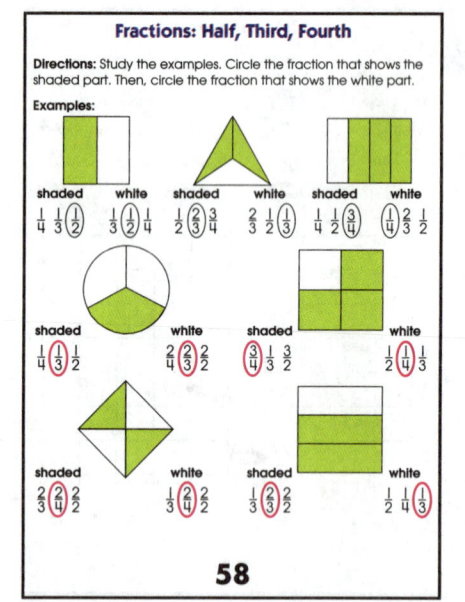

Fractions: Half, Third, Fourth

Directions: Study the examples. Circle the fraction that shows the shaded part. Then, circle the fraction that shows the white part.

Examples:

58

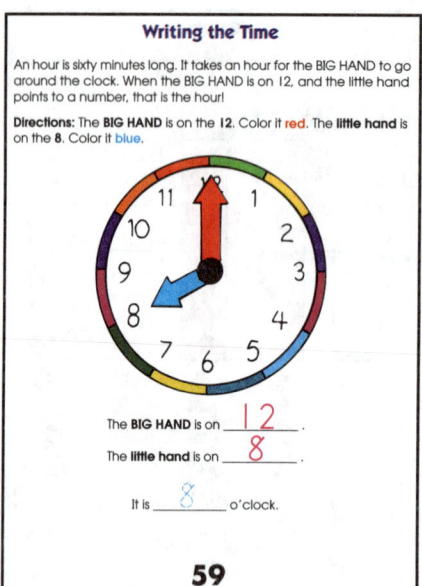

Writing the Time

An hour is sixty minutes long. It takes an hour for the BIG HAND to go around the clock. When the BIG HAND is on 12, and the little hand points to a number, that is the hour!

Directions: The BIG HAND is on the 12. Color it red. The little hand is on the 8. Color it blue.

The BIG HAND is on __12__.
The little hand is on __8__.
It is __8__ o'clock.

59

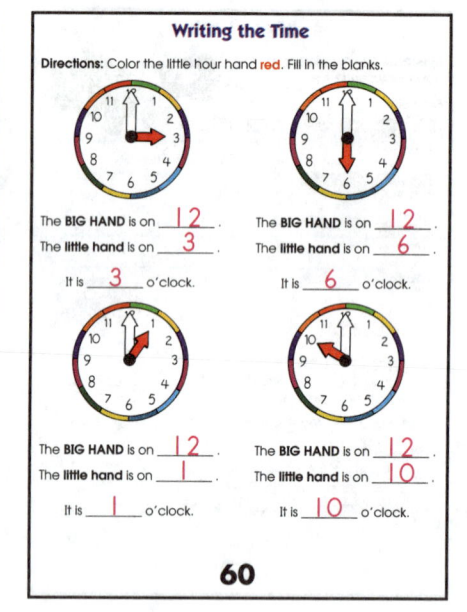

Writing the Time

Directions: Color the little hour hand red. Fill in the blanks.

The BIG HAND is on __12__.
The little hand is on __3__.
It is __3__ o'clock.

The BIG HAND is on __12__.
The little hand is on __6__.
It is __6__ o'clock.

The BIG HAND is on __12__.
The little hand is on __1__.
It is __1__ o'clock.

The BIG HAND is on __12__.
The little hand is on __10__.
It is __10__ o'clock.

60

Math: Grade 2 78 ©2006 Carson-Dellosa Publishing

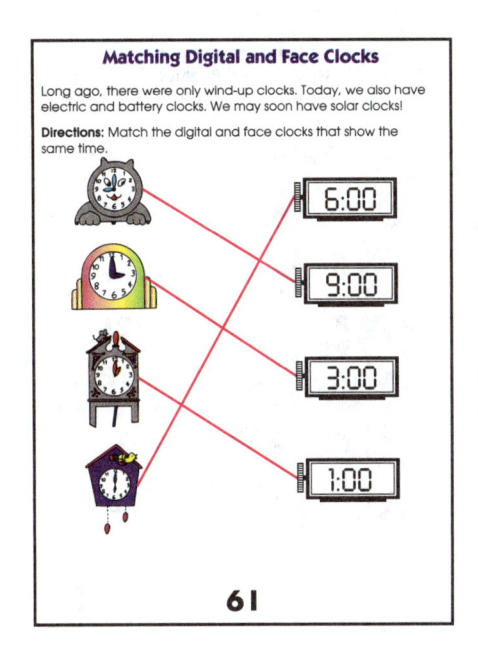

Matching Digital and Face Clocks

Long ago, there were only wind-up clocks. Today, we also have electric and battery clocks. We may soon have solar clocks!

Directions: Match the digital and face clocks that show the same time.

- 6:00
- 9:00
- 3:00
- 1:00

61

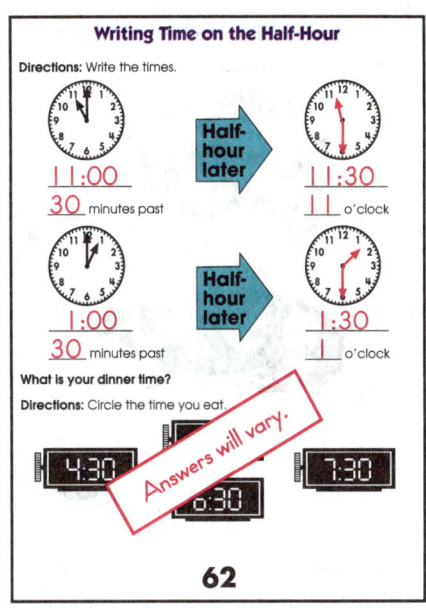

Writing Time on the Half-Hour

Directions: Write the times.

11:00
30 minutes past
→ Half-hour later →
11:30
11 o'clock

1:00
30 minutes past
→ Half-hour later →
1:30
1 o'clock

What is your dinner time?
Directions: Circle the time you eat.

Answers will vary.

62

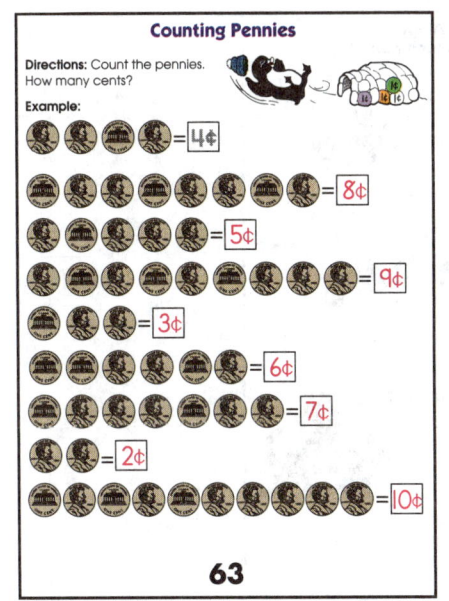

Counting Pennies

Directions: Count the pennies. How many cents?

Example:
= 4¢
= 8¢
= 5¢
= 9¢
= 3¢
= 6¢
= 7¢
= 2¢
= 10¢

63

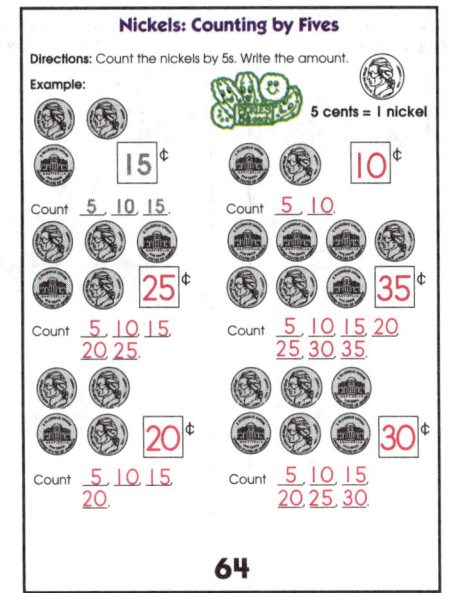

Nickels: Counting by Fives

Directions: Count the nickels by 5s. Write the amount.

Example:
5 cents = 1 nickel

15¢   10¢
Count 5, 10, 15.   Count 5, 10.

25¢   35¢
Count 5, 10, 15,   Count 5, 10, 15, 20,
20, 25.   25, 30, 35.

20¢   30¢
Count 5, 10, 15,   Count 5, 10, 15,
20.   20, 25, 30.

64

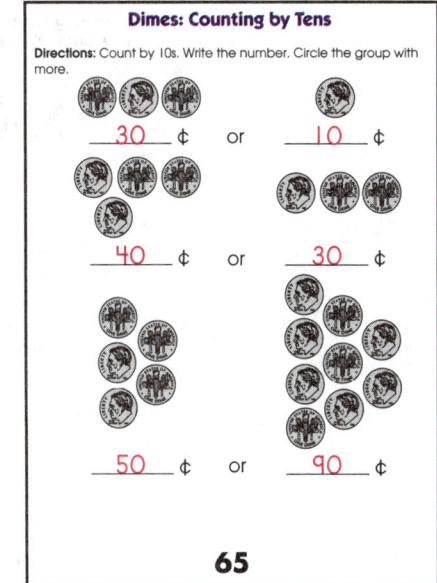

Dimes: Counting by Tens

Directions: Count by 10s. Write the number. Circle the group with more.

30 ¢   or   10 ¢

40 ¢   or   30 ¢

50 ¢   or   90 ¢

65

79

Math: Grade 2

Counting With Dimes, Nickels, and Pennies

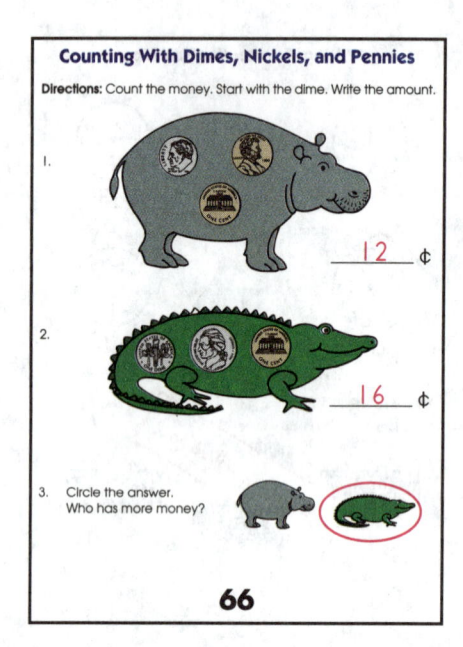

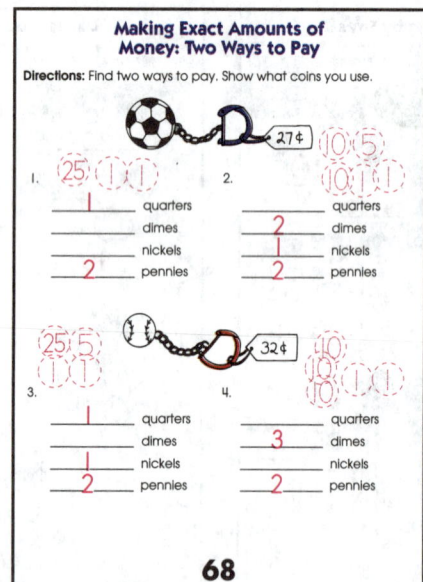

Directions: Count the money. Start with the dime. Write the amount.

1. ___12___ ¢

2. ___16___ ¢

3. Circle the answer. Who has more money? (alligator circled)

66

Counting With Quarters, Dimes, Nickels, and Pennies

Directions: Match the money with the amount.

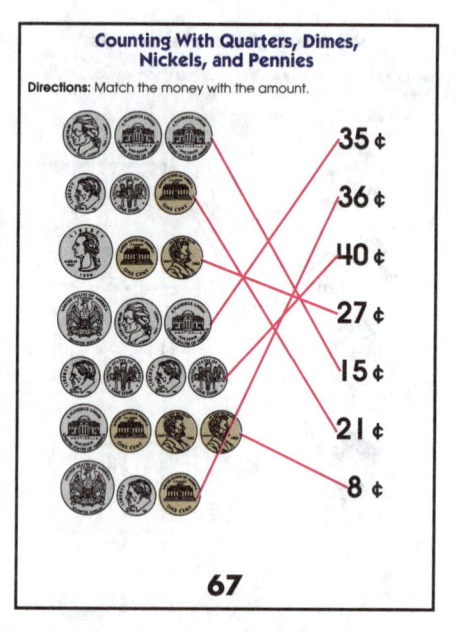

35 ¢
36 ¢
40 ¢
27 ¢
15 ¢
21 ¢
8 ¢

67

Making Exact Amounts of Money: Two Ways to Pay

Directions: Find two ways to pay. Show what coins you use.

27¢

1. (25)(1)(1)
   ___ quarters
   _1_ dimes
   ___ nickels
   _2_ pennies

2. (10)(5)(10)(1)(1)
   ___ quarters
   _2_ dimes
   _1_ nickels
   _2_ pennies

32¢

3. (25)(5)(1)(1)
   ___ quarters
   _1_ dimes
   ___ nickels
   _2_ pennies

4. (10)(10)(10)
   ___ quarters
   _3_ dimes
   ___ nickels
   _2_ pennies

68

Making Exact Amounts of Money: How Much More?

Directions: Count the coins. Find out how much more money you need to pay the exact amount.

50¢

How much money do you have? ___25___ ¢
How much more money do you need? ___25___ ¢

60¢

How much money do you have? ___11___ ¢
How much more money do you need? ___49___ ¢

Solve this puzzle.
How much more money does Monkey need?

I have 1 quarter and 4 dimes. I need one more coin to pay for the banana-van.

75¢

___10___ ¢

69

Math: Grade 2 — 80 — ©2006 Carson-Dellosa Publishing